PRIMARY MATHEMATICS

Standards Edition

TESTS

Charlene Riaz

Marshall Cavendish Education

SM SingaporeMath.com Inc®

Preface

Primary Mathematics (Standards Edition) Tests is a series of assessment books

This series is aligned with the standards adopted by the California State Board of Education and follows the topical arrangement in the Primary Mathematics (Standards Edition) Textbooks. Each chapter comprises Test A and Test B, and each unit concludes with similarly structured Cumulative Tests.

Test A consists of free response questions and assesses students' grasp of mathematical concepts while developing problem-solving skills. Test B is optional and consists of multiple-choice questions aimed at testing students' comprehension of key concepts. As such, it may be used as a retest if teachers perceive the need.

In Cumulative Tests A and B, questions from earlier units are incorporated into each test. These tests focus on review and consolidation through the integration of concepts and strands.

Primary Mathematics (Standards Edition) Tests aims to provide teachers with a set of structured assessment tools for the systematic evaluation of students' learning so as to better understand their individual needs.

Contents

20

Test A

Unit 1: Numbers to 10,000

Chapter 1: Thousands, Hundreds, Tens and Ones

Write the expanded form of the number shown below.

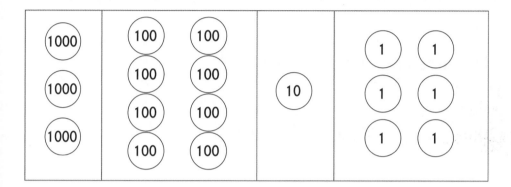

_____

$2075 = 2000 +$ _____

Write in words.

7035 _____

Write in standard form.

one thousand, two _____

Count on and fill in the blanks with the missing numbers.

3426, 3427, 3428, _____, _____

1

6. In the number 6149,

    (a) the digit _____ is in the thousands place.

    (b) the value of the digit 1 is _____.

    (c) the digit 4 is in the _____ place.

7. Fill in each ◯ with **>** or **<**.

    2056 ◯ 1978 ◯ 1263

8. Write the missing digit in the box.

    7 ☐ 26 < 7126

9. What is the greatest 4-digit number that you can make
    using the digits 4, 1, 7 and 0?
    (Use each digit only once. Do not begin the number with 0

    _____

10. Arrange the numbers in order.
    Begin with the smallest.

    1329, 2329, 1293, 897

    _____

. Write all the different 3-digit numbers you can make with the digits below.

| 3 | 7 | 2 |

_____

. (a) Use the digits below to make four different 4-digit numbers.
   (Use each digit only once for each number.)

| 6 | 2 | 8 | 3 |

_____   _____

_____   _____

(b) Arrange the numbers in order.
    Begin with the greatest.

_____

Blank

Test B

Unit 1: Numbers to 10,000

Chapter 1: Thousands, Hundreds, Tens and Ones

Circle the correct option, **A**, **B**, **C** or **D**.

Which number comes next?

8995, 8996, 8997, 8998, 8999, _____

  A   8000   **C**   9000

  B   8990   **D**   10,000

3208 in words is _____.

  A   three hundred twenty-eight

  B   three hundred, two hundred eight

  C   three thousand, twenty-eight

  D   three thousand, two hundred eight

What is five thousand, two hundred twelve in expanded form?

  A   5 + 2 + 1 + 2   **C**   5000 + 100 + 20 + 2

  B   5200 + 120 + 0   **D**   5000 + 200 + 10 + 2

What is 6 thousands and 4 tens in standard form?

  A   6004   **C**   6400

  B   6040   **D**   600,040

© 2008 Marshall Cavendish International (Singapore) Private Limited   Primary Mathematics (Standards Edition) Tests 3A

5. Which digit in the number 5724 is in the thousands place?

    A   5   **C**   2

    B   7   **D**   4

6. Which of the following is **not** true?

    A   395 < 1000   **C**   1746 > 936

    B   805 > 794   **D**   9045 < 5940

7. Which of the following is the greatest number?

    A   8005   **C**   5380

    B   5832   **D**   976

8. Which number belongs in the box?

    3627 > ⬚ > 805

    A   85   **C**   6345

    B   1783   **D**   9000

9. How many different 3-digit numbers can you make using the digits 4, 1 and 6?
   (Use each digit only once for each number.)

    A   1   **C**   6

    B   4   **D**   8

10. Which set of numbers is arranged in order from the smallest?

    A   1136, 1162, 2145, 915   **C**   915, 1136, 1162, 2145

    B   2145, 1162, 1136, 915   **D**   915, 1162, 1136, 2145

Primary Mathematics (Standards Edition) Tests 3A

© 2008 Marshall Cavendish International (Singapore) Private Lim

Test A

Unit 1: Numbers to 10,000

Chapter 2: Number Patterns

10 more than 3397 is _____.

Compare the two numbers and answer the following questions.

| 1725 | | 725 |

(a) Which is smaller?
Circle the correct answer.

(b) How much smaller?

_____ is _____ less than _____.

_____ is 1000 more than 9000.

1000 less than 8402 is _____.

Nathan counted on in steps of 100's until he reached the number below.
Fill in the blanks with the numbers he counted.

3560

_____   _____   _____

100   100

08 Marshall Cavendish International (Singapore) Private Limited   Primary Mathematics (Standards Edition) Tests 3A

6. I think of a number.
   It is 100 less than 4000.

   What is the number? _____

7. The year is 2008.
   10 years ago, it was 1998.

   100 years ago, it was _____.

8. Mary paid $1247 for a television set.
   Lily paid $100 less than Mary for her television set.
   How much did Lily pay for her television set?

   Lily paid $_____.

9. Alan had $5216 in his bank account in January.
   He put in $1000 the next month.
   How much did he have in his bank account in February?

   He had $_____.

Primary Mathematics (Standards Edition) Tests 3A   © 2008 Marshall Cavendish International (Singapore) Private Lim

0. Write the missing numbers in the boxes.

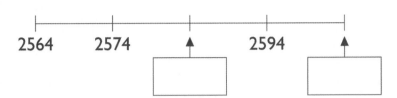

2564   2574   2594

1. Write the missing numbers in the boxes.

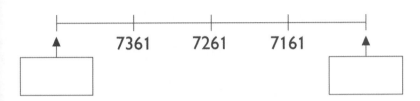

7361   7261   7161

2. Fill in the blanks with the numbers in the boxes.

3075   100   2975

_____ more than _____ is _____.

Blank

Test B

Unit 1: Numbers to 10,000

Chapter 2: Number Patterns

Circle the correct option, **A**, **B**, **C** or **D**.

Which number is 1000 less than 8512?

A 7512 **B** 8412 **C** 8502 **D** 9512

1 more than **2639** is _____.

A 2640 **B** 2649 **C** 2739 **D** 3639

Sally has $9900 and Jim has $100 more than Sally.
How much does Jim have?

A $8900 **B** $9000 **C** $9800 **D** $10,000

Count backwards in a regular pattern. What comes next?

3815, 2815, 1815, _____

A 815 **B** 1805 **C** 1915 **D** 4815

Count by 100's from 2317.

The fifth number after 2317 is _____.

A 2217 **B** 2517 **C** 2817 **D** 3017

Which numbers belong in the boxes?

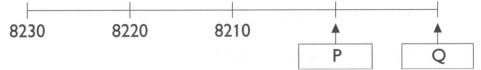

8230   8220   8210   P   Q

A P: 8220, Q: 8230 **C** P: 8200, Q: 8190

B P: 8110, Q: 8010 **D** P: 8200, Q: 7200

11

7. Which of the following shows counting by 1000's?

    A   5261, 6361, 7461, 8561

    B   7418, 6418, 5418, 4418

    C   9010, 9110, 9210, 9310

    D   3995, 4005, 4015, 4025

8. Mr. Chan's table cost $816.
   Mr. Lee's table cost $1000 more than Mr. Chan's table.
   Mr. Kim's table cost $100 more than Mr. Lee's table.
   How much did Mr. Kim's table cost?

    A $916   C $1826

    B $1816   D $1916

9. Kelly counted by 10's from 2658.
   She made a mistake in one of the numbers.
   Which number was it?

   2658, 2768, 2678, 2688, 2698

    A   2678   C   2698

    B   2688   D   2768

10. Which sentence is correct?

    A   100 less than 5192 is 5292.

    B   1000 more than 219 is 319.

    C   3607 is 10 more than 3597.

    D   9999 is 1 more than 10,000.

Primary Mathematics (Standards Edition) Tests 3A   © 2008 Marshall Cavendish International (Singapore) Private Li

Unit 1: Numbers to 10,000

Chapter 3: Rounding Numbers

(a) Draw an arrow to the point on the number line where the number 41 should be.

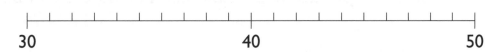

30   40   50

(b)   41 rounded to the nearest ten is _____.

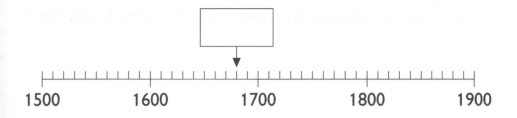

1500   1600   1700   1800   1900

(a) What is the missing number in the box? _____

(b) Round the number to the nearest hundred. _____

578 rounded to the nearest hundred is _____.

Round 7195 to the nearest ten. _____

4129 rounded to the nearest hundred is _____.

6. Round 2956 to the nearest hundred. _____

7. 8674 rounded to the nearest thousand is _____.

8. A number rounded to the nearest ten is 60.
   What is the **greatest** possible number that it can be?

   _____

9. A number rounded to the nearest hundred is 1300.
   What is the **smallest** possible number that it can be?

   _____

10. Write a number that can be rounded to 720.

    _____

11. 7694 rounded to the nearest _____ is 8000.

12. A number rounded to the nearest thousand is 5000.
    The number has the digit 5 in the hundreds place and the
    digit 4 in the ones place.
    What is a possible number?
    Write the missing digits in the boxes below.

    ☐ 5 ☐ 4

Primary Mathematics (Standards Edition) Tests 3A   © 2008 Marshall Cavendish International (Singapore) Private L

Test B   Unit 1: Numbers to 10,000

Chapter 3: Rounding Numbers

Circle the correct option, **A**, **B**, **C** or **D**.

Name the tens before and after 37.

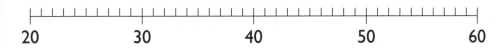

20   30   40   50   60

The number 37 is between _____.

A	20 and 30	**C**	40 and 50
B	30 and 40	**D**	50 and 60

37 rounded to the nearest ten is _____.

A	30	**C**	50
B	40	**D**	100

Round 1754 to the nearest hundred.

A	1600	**C**	1750
B	1700	**D**	1800

Round 1473 to the nearest thousand.

A	1000	**C**	1500
B	1470	**D**	2000

5. Which number is 8400 when rounded to the nearest hundre

    A   8348   **C**   8467

    B   8432   **D**   8501

6. Round 9996 to the nearest ten.

    A   9000   **C**   9990

    B   9900   **D**   10,000

7. This number is 7000 when rounded to the nearest thousand What is the **smallest** possible number that it can be?

    A   7001   **C**   7502

    B   6501   **D**   6999

8. This number is 5100 when rounded to the nearest hundre What is the **greatest** possible number that it can be?

    A   5209   **C**   5099

    B   5149   **D**   5050

9. Which number is **not** 7190 when rounded to the nearest te

    A   7185   **C**   7192

    B   7188   **D**   7195

10. 6548 is 6500 rounded to the nearest _____.

    A   one   **C**   hundred

    B   ten   **D**   thousand

Primary Mathematics (Standards Edition) Tests 3A   © 2008 Marshall Cavendish International (Singapore) Private Lir

Cumulative Test A **Unit 1**

Write the number in words.

7520

_____

Write in standard form.

two thousand, four hundred eleven _____

Write the number in expanded form.

6708

_____

What is the number shown below? _____

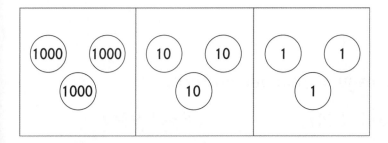

The value of the digit **8** in **8674** is _____.

6. Write a 4-digit number with the digit 2 in the tens place and the digit 9 in the thousands place.

   _____

7. Fill in each ( ) with > or <.

   862 ( ) 981 ( ) 1000

8. What is the greatest 4-digit number? _____

9. Arrange the numbers in order.
   Begin with the greatest.

   8527, 2857, 8572, 2785

   _____

10. Write a number that is greater than 4709 but smaller tho
    4970.

    _____

11. Complete the regular number pattern.

    _____, 5347, 6347, _____, 8347, 9347

2. Complete the regular number pattern.

7048, 7038, 7028, _____, _____

3. Count by 100's from 7925.
What is the third number after 7925? _____

4. Factory A made 2562 cans of beans.
Factory B made 100 fewer cans than Factory A.
Factory C made 10 more cans than Factory B.
How many cans of beans did Factory C make?

Factory C made _____ cans of beans.

. Look at the number line below.

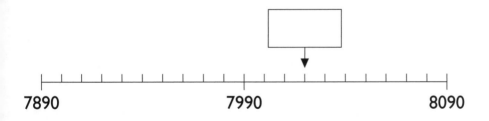

7890   7990   8090

(a) What is the missing number in the box? _____

(b) Round the number to the nearest hundred. _____

16. 8673 rounded to the nearest ten is _____.

17. Round 7269 to the nearest thousand. _____

18. 12 hundreds, 12 tens and 12 ones is _____.

19. A number is made up of the digits in the boxes.
It is 3000 when rounded to the nearest thousand.
What is the **smallest** possible number that it can be?
What is the **greatest** possible number that it can be?
(Use each digit only once.)

| 5 | 3 | 2 | 6 |

Smallest number: _____

Greatest number: _____

Primary Mathematics (Standards Edition) Tests 3A   © 2008 Marshall Cavendish International (Singapore) Private Li

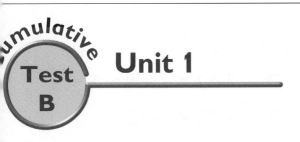

Cumulative Test B **Unit 1**

Circle the correct option, **A**, **B**, **C** or **D**.

What is 3715 in words?

A   three thousand, seven hundred, ten and five

B   three thousand, seventy-one hundred five

C   three thousand, seven hundred fifteen

D   thirty-seven thousand, fifteen

What is 9236 in expanded form?

A   92 + 36   **C**   6000 + 300 + 20 + 9

B   9 + 20 + 300 + 6000   **D**   9000 + 200 + 30 + 6

What is the **smallest** 4-digit number?

A   999   **C**   101

B   1000   **D**   1001

What is the value of the digit 5 in the number 7529?

A   5   **C**   500

B   50   **D**   5000

Which number has the digit 7 in the hundreds place?

A   1076   **C**   7319

B   5637   **D**   8712

21

6. Which statement is correct?

   A   75 > 705   **C**   7452 = 7 + 4 + 5 + 2

   B   999 < 1000   **D**   3472 < 3422

7. Which set of numbers is arranged in order from the greates

   A   594, 890, 1526, 7327

   B   2076, 2067, 1987, 1026

   C   9730, 3562, 4026, 257

   D   6147, 7147, 8147, 9147

8. What number is 10 less than 300?

   A   200   **C**   299

   B   290   **D**   310

9. What number is 100 more than 1936?

   A   1836   **C**   2036

   B   1935   **D**   2936

10. What is the missing number in the number pattern?

    3726, 3826, _____, 4026

    A   3626   **C**   4026

    B   3926   **D**   4826

11. Look at the following sets of numbers.
    Which set has a number that is 100 more than the
    other number?

    A   1396 and 1406   **C**   3629 and 3630

    B   1783 and 1883   **D**   8421 and 9421

Primary Mathematics (Standards Edition) Tests 3A

. The year is 2987.
10 years later, it will be 2997.
100 years later, it will be _____.

A   2887   C   3087

B   3007   D   3997

. 8427 rounded to the nearest ten is _____.

A   8400   C   8430

B   8420   D   8440

. 8963 rounded to the nearest hundred is _____.

A   8000   C   8960

B   8900   D   9000

. Round 4347 to the nearest thousand.

A   4000   C   4400

B   4300   D   5000

. Which number is **not** 6500 when rounded to the nearest ten?

A   6496   C   6501

B   6499   D   6512

. A number is 3200 when rounded to the nearest hundred.
Which of the following numbers is it?

A   2376   C   3267

B   3172   D   3621

18. Jason has 2514 coins.
    Sarwan has 1000 more coins than Jason.
    Cindy has 100 fewer coins than Jason.
    How many coins does Cindy have?

    A   2614   C   3514

    B   3414   D   3614

19. Which digits must be placed in the thousands and hundre
    places so that the number below is 10,000 when rounded
    to the nearest 1000?

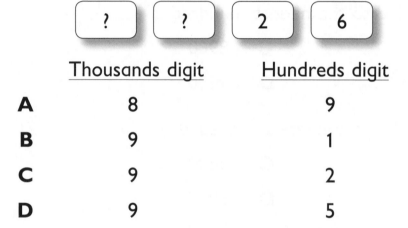

	Thousands digit	Hundreds digit
A	8	9
B	9	1
C	9	2
D	9	5

20. Which number will give the same answer when rounded t
    the nearest ten or to the nearest hundred?

    A   2504   C   4652

    B   3942   D   9985

Test A

Unit 2: Addition and Subtraction

Chapter 1: Mental Calculation

$58 +$ _____ $= 60$

Add 92 and 7. _____

What number is 6 more than 25? _____

Add 65 and 13. _____

What number is 50 more than 37? _____

Subtract 50 from 92. _____

Subtract 4 from 20. _____

Subtract 7 from 35. _____

Subtract 9 from 42. _____

. What is $46 + 18$? _____

. What is $53 + 37$? _____

. Add 12 and 69. _____

. Add 78 and 46. _____

14. Subtract 43 from 72. _____

15. Subtract 18 from 164. _____

16. Subtract 26 from 300. _____

17. Subtract 3 tens from 60. _____

18. $628 - 300 =$ _____

19. $84 - 39 =$ _____

20. $360 - 28 =$ _____

21. $283 + 97 =$ _____

22. $675 - 98 =$ _____

23. _____ $+ 27 = 85$

Primary Mathematics (Standards Edition) Tests 3A

4. Add 15, 26, 32 and 18.
   Show your working below.

   The answer is _____.

5. What is the value of 12 + 53 + 37 + 48?
   Show your working below.

   The answer is _____.

Blank

Test B

Unit 2: Addition and Subtraction

Chapter 1: Mental Calculation

Circle the correct option, **A**, **B**, **C** or **D**.

What is 20 + 64?

A   24

C   84

B   26

D   94

Subtract 6 from 20.

A   14

C   26

B   24

D   80

Add 55 and 36.

A   39

C   81

B   41

D   91

Subtract 22 from 95.

A   67

C   77

B   73

D   167

Add 106 and 7.

A   101

C   176

B   113

D   906

Turn the page.

6. What is 48 – 19?

   A 29   C 39

   B 31   D 57

7. What is 217 – 17?

   A 47   C 220

   B 200   D 234

8. What is 147 + 98?

   A 47   C 245

   B 49   D 247

9. Find the value of 20 + 16 + 43 + 67.

   A 46   C 146

   B 136   D 1316

10. Add 12, 17, 38 and 42.

   A 29   C 97

   B 80   D 109

Primary Mathematics (Standards Edition) Tests 3A

© 2008 Marshall Cavendish International (Singapore) Private Li

Test A

Unit 2: Addition and Subtraction

Chapter 2: Sum and Difference

What is the sum of 9 and 6? _____

Find the difference between 2 and 8. _____

Find the sum of 37 and 22. _____

32 more than 68 is _____.

Find the difference between 48 and 36. _____

$47 +$ _____ $= 54$

The sum of two numbers is 90.
One number is 37.
The other number is _____.

32 less than _____ is 10.

Fill in the $\bigcirc$ with **+** or **−**.

$81 \bigcirc 26 = 55$

© Marshall Cavendish International (Singapore) Private Limited

Primary Mathematics (Standards Edition) Tests 3A

10. Fill in the blanks.

(a) 32 + _____ = 71 (b) _____ + 12 = 30

(c) 94 − _____ = 23 (d) _____ − 28 = 60

11. Compare the two numbers and fill in the blanks.

62 and 26

(a) Which number is greater? _____

(b) _____ is _____ more than _____.

12. Fill in each ◯ with **+** or **−**.

27 ◯ 43 < 61 ◯ 29

13. Fill in each ◯ with **>**, **<** or **=**.

(a) 14 + 82 ◯ 97 − 68

(b) 23 + 59 ◯ 41 + 41

(c) 89 − 67 ◯ 13 + 9

(d) 35 − 9 ◯ 86 − 49 ◯ 16 + 28

Test B

Unit 2: Addition and Subtraction

Chapter 2: Sum and Difference

Circle the correct option, **A**, **B**, **C** or **D**.

What is the sum of 5 and 6?

A   1   **C**   30

B   11   **D**   56

What is the difference between 2 and 9?

A   7   **C**   18

B   11   **D**   29

May did the following addition problem.

$$\begin{array}{r} 5\ 9 \\ +\ 1\ 8 \\ \hline 7\ 7 \end{array}$$

Which of these will help her check if she is correct?

A   77 + 18   **C**   59 + 77

B   77 − 18   **D**   18 + 59 + 77

Which sign belongs in the ⬭?

15 ⬭ 68 = 83

A   >   **C**   −

B   <   **D**   +

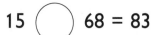

5. The sum of two numbers is 42.
   One of the numbers is 18.
   What is the other number?

   A 24   **C** 78

   B 60   **D** 102

6. Which sign belongs in each ( )?

   68 ( ) 12 ( ) 80

   A −, =   **C** −, >

   B +, =   **D** +, <

7. Which of the following must you do to find the missing number in the box?

   43 + ☐ = 61

   A 43 − 61   **C** 43 + 43

   B 61 − 43   **D** 43 + 61

8. Which number belongs in the box?

   ☐ − 37 = 19

   A 18   **C** 28

   B 22   **D** 56

Primary Mathematics (Standards Edition) Tests 3A

Which sentence is correct?

A   25 is 17 less than 40.

B   47 is 15 more than 62.

C   50 is 20 less than 30.

D   61 is 36 more than 25.

0. 23 more than ☐ is 70.

Which number belongs in the box?

A   47   C   57

B   53   D   93

. ☐ less than 35 is 16.

Which number belongs in the box?

A   19   C   29

B   21   D   54

2. 45 more than 19 is ☐.

Which number belongs in the box?

A   26   C   54

B   34   D   64

. Which sign belongs in the ◯?

55 + 17 ◯ 83 − 19

A   >   C   <

B   =   D   +

14. Which sign belongs in each ( )?

60 ( ) 18 < 46 ( ) 17

    A   +, +   **C**   +, −

    B   −, +   **D**   −, −

15. Find the sum of 26 and 47.
    Subtract 35 from the sum.
    What do you get?

    A   38   **C**   71

    B   61   **D**   106

Test A

Unit 2: Addition and Subtraction

Chapter 3: Estimation

Find the sum of 68 and 49.
Use estimation to check if your answer is reasonable.

$$\begin{array}{r} 6\ 8 \\ +\ 4\ 9 \\ \hline \end{array}$$

Estimation

Is your answer reasonable? _____

Find the difference between 83 and 69.
Use estimation to check if your answer is reasonable.

$$\begin{array}{r} 8\ 3 \\ -\ 6\ 9 \\ \hline \end{array}$$

Estimation

Is your answer reasonable? _____

3. Estimate the sum of 247 and 512 by rounding each number to the nearest hundred.

Estimation

The answer is about _____.

4. Alisha did the addition problem 265 + 48 = 745.
Round 265 to the nearest hundred and 48 to the nearest
Then use estimation to check if her answer is reasonable.

Estimation

Is her answer reasonable? _____

5. Alan has $379.
Walter has $435 more than Alan.
Estimate the amount Walter has. $_____

Primary Mathematics (Standards Edition) Tests 3A

Estimate the difference between 763 and 321.

The answer should be about _____.

Subtract 57 from 893.
Use addition to check if your answer is correct.

Addition

The answer is _____.

What is 163 + 400 + 299?
Use estimation to check if your answer is reasonable.

Estimation

Is your answer reasonable? _____

What is 35 more than 658? _____

Is the answer closer to 600 or 700? _____

10. Betty did the following estimation.

    300 − 100 = 200

    The question was 3 ⬜ 6 − 97.

    What could the number in the box be? _____

11. Find the actual value of the following.
    Use estimation to check if your answer is reasonable.

    65 + 24 + 17 + 89 = _____

Estimation

    Is your answer reasonable? _____

12. Fill in the blank with the missing number.
    Use estimation to check if the answer is reasonable.

    631 − _____ = 228

Estimation

    Is the answer reasonable? _____

Test B

Unit 2: Addition and Subtraction

Chapter 3: Estimation

Circle the correct option, **A**, **B**, **C** or **D**.

Estimate the sum of 615 and 32.

A	600 + 30	**C**	700 + 30
B	600 + 40	**D**	700 + 40

Estimate the value of 328 + 495.

A	700	**C**	900
B	800	**D**	1000

Estimate the value of 652 + 94.
Which of the following is the closest estimate?

A	600 + 90	**C**	700 + 90
B	600 + 100	**D**	700 + 100

Estimate the value of 792 – 283.

A	700 – 200	**C**	800 – 200
B	700 – 300	**D**	800 – 300

Find the difference between 600 and 323.

A	277	**C**	377
B	323	**D**	923

6. Lily found the difference between 708 and 119.
   Which should she use to check if her answer is reasonabl

   A 700 – 100   C 800 – 100

   B 700 – 200   D 800 – 200

7. The sum of 78 and 65 is about _____.
   Estimate the answer by rounding 78 and 65 to the nearest te

   A 120   C 140

   B 130   D 150

8. Estimate the difference between 521 and 296.

   A 200   C 400

   B 300   D 800

9. Henry estimated his answer to an addition problem as
   300 + 600.
   Which of the following problems was he doing?

   A 286 + 557   C 375 + 615

   B 318 + 542   D 398 + 673

10. Estimate the value of 417 – 363 by rounding both number
    to the nearest ten.

    A 0   C 50

    B 40   D 60

Test A

Unit 2: Addition and Subtraction

Chapter 4: Word Problems

Solve the following word problems. You may draw models to help you.

735 mugs were made in a factory on Monday.
On Tuesday, 409 mugs were made.
How many mugs were made altogether?

_____ mugs were made altogether.

Mrs. Wang bought 721 cans of baked beans.
She sold 163 cans.
How many cans did she have left?

She had _____ cans left.

Julio scored 900 points in a game.
He lost 563 points in the next game.
How many points did he have left?

He had _____ points left.

© 2008 Marshall Cavendish International (Singapore) Private Limited

4. Mrs. Brown made 45 buns on Monday, 25 buns on Tuesday, 37 buns on Wednesday and 41 buns on Thursday.
How many buns did she make altogether?

She made _____ buns altogether.

5. Jill has $276.
She has $95 more than Jack.
How much does Jack have?

Jack has $_____.

6. There are 321 men and 186 women at a school concert.

(a) How many adults are there?

There are _____ adults.

(b) There are 100 more children than adults at the concert.
How many children are there?

There are _____ children.

Primary Mathematics (Standards Edition) Tests 3A   © 2008 Marshall Cavendish International (Singapore) Private Lim

Harold has 603 stamps in his collection.
Dan has 215 fewer stamps than Harold.

(a) How many stamps does Dan have?

Dan has _____ stamps.

(b) How many stamps do they have altogether?

They have _____ stamps altogether.

I have 845 sheets of paper.
I use 628 sheets of paper to print some labels.

(a) How many sheets of paper do I have left?

I have _____ sheets of paper left.

(b) I need 521 sheets of paper to print more labels.
How many more sheets of paper do I need?

I need _____ more sheets of paper.

9. Susan sold 168 cards on the first day she opened her shop and had 259 cards left.

    (a) How many cards did she have at first?

    She had _____ cards at first.

    (b) If she sold 96 cards on the second day, how many cards did she have left?

    She had _____ cards left.

10. Mr. Luigi had to print 185 cards.
    He printed 42 cards in the morning and 76 cards in the afternoon.

    (a) How many cards did he print altogether?

    He printed _____ cards altogether.

    (b) How many more cards did he have to print?

    He had to print _____ more cards.

Test B

Unit 2: Addition and Subtraction

Chapter 4: Word Problems

Circle the correct option, **A**, **B**, **C** or **D**.

Latifa read 59 books last year.
She read 12 more books this year.
How many books did she read this year?

A   43   **C**   61

B   47   **D**   71

A machine made 275 biscuits in the morning.
It made 25 fewer biscuits in the afternoon.
How many biscuits did it make in the afternoon?

A   250   **C**   525

B   300   **D**   575

Mr. Smith spent $615 on transport and $26 less on food.
How much did he spend on food?

A $355   **C** $611

B $589   **D** $641

Joshua has 183 stickers.
He has 95 more stickers than Matthew.
How many stickers does Matthew have?

A   88   **C**   278

B   112   **D**   767

5. A handbag cost $560.
   At a sale, it cost $375.
   How much less did the bag cost at the sale?

   A $115   C $185

   B $150   D $215

6. Alice has to type an essay.
   She has typed 349 words.
   She still has 573 more words to type.
   How many words are there in her essay?
   Which of the following shows the number sentence for
   this problem?

   A $\boxed{} + 349 = 573$ C $573 - 349 = \boxed{}$

   B $573 + 349 = \boxed{}$ D $573 - \boxed{} = 349$

7. Sam had $950 in the bank.
   He took out $525.
   How much money did he have left in the bank?

   A $249   C $601

   B $425   D $1651

8. Karen bought 112 blue marbles, 80 purple marbles and
   9 red marbles.
   How many marbles did she buy altogether?

   A   23   C   201

   B   47   D   1812

Primary Mathematics (Standards Edition) Tests 3A   © 2008 Marshall Cavendish International (Singapore) Private Li

There are 27 students in the blue team, 34 students in the green team and 19 students in the yellow team.
How many students are there altogether?

A   46   C   61

B   53   D   80

0. Felix scored the following points for his tests.

English	82
Math	76
Science	?
Total	248

What was his score for the Science test?

A   6   C   90

B   48   D   158

Blank

Test A

Unit 2: Addition and Subtraction

Chapter 5: Adding Ones, Tens, Hundreds and Thousands

Find the sum of 1628 and 6.
Show your working below.

What is 50 more than 2763?
Show your working below.

Write the missing digit in each box.

```
  3 6 5 2              5 4 3 2
+   □ 0              +    8 □
---------            ---------
  3 7 1 2              5 5 2 1
```

Primary Mathematics (Standards Edition) Tests 3A

4. What is the sum of 6241 and 2826?
   Show your working below.

5. Find the sum of 2073 and 3947.
   Show your working below.

6. Zac added 7685 to 1246 as shown.

$$
\begin{array}{r}
7\,6\,8\,5 \\
+\ 1\,2\,4\,6 \\
\hline
8\,9\,3\,1
\end{array}
$$

   Round 7685 and 1246 to the nearest thousand to check if
   his answer is reasonable.

   Estimation

   Is his answer reasonable? _____

Primary Mathematics (Standards Edition) Tests 3A
© 2008 Marshall Cavendish International (Singapore) Private Li

Round 478 and 655 to the nearest hundred to check if the answer is reasonable.

478 + 655 = 1133

Estimation

Is the answer reasonable? _____

Round 5269 and 3948 to the nearest hundred to check if the answer is reasonable.

5269 + 3948 = 9217

Estimation

Is the answer reasonable? _____

What would you do to check if the following addition problem is correct?
Circle the correct answer.

$$
\begin{array}{r}
3\,6\,2\,7 \\
+\,3\,9\,9\,8 \\
\hline
7\,6\,2\,5
\end{array}
$$

7625 + 3998   7625 + 3627   7625 − 3998

). Write the missing digit in the box.

$$
\begin{array}{r}
9\,9\,9\,6 \\
+\quad\square \\
\hline
1\,0,0\,0\,0
\end{array}
$$

11. (a) Form the **greatest** and the **smallest** 4-digit numbers using all the digits below.
Use each digit only once for each number.

3, 4, 1, 6

Greatest number: _____

Smallest number: _____

(b) Add the two numbers.

The sum of the two numbers is _____.

12. Mary estimated the answer to an addition problem as shown below.

$$\begin{array}{r} 2\,0\,0\,0 \\ +\,5\,0\,0\,0 \\ \hline 7\,0\,0\,0 \end{array}$$

Which one of these addition problems was she estimating

Check ✔ the correct answer.

1834 + 4727 = 6561 ☐

2599 + 5681 = 8280 ☐

Primary Mathematics (Standards Edition) Tests 3A

© 2008 Marshall Cavendish International (Singapore) Private Lir

Test B

Unit 2: Addition and Subtraction

Chapter 5: Adding Ones, Tens, Hundreds and Thousands

Circle the correct option, **A**, **B**, **C** or **D**.

Find the sum of 5 and 2178.

A	2183	**C**	2678
B	2228	**D**	7178

Which number belongs in the box?

$$
\begin{array}{r}
8\ 3\ 2\ 9 \\
+\quad\square \\
\hline
8\ 3\ 3\ 6
\end{array}
$$

A	1	**C**	5
B	3	**D**	7

What is 60 more than 2059?

A	2119	**C**	4178
B	2659	**D**	8059

What is 400 more than 5279?

A	4879	**C**	9479
B	5679	**D**	9679

5. Put together 1476 Thailand stamps and 586 Singapore stamp[s].
How many stamps are there?

   A   890   C   2648

   B   2062   D   4384

6. Patrick has $5625.
Yati has $1385 more than Patrick.
How much does Yati have?

   A $4240   C $7000

   B $6900   D $7010

7. Which of the following addition problems gives the
answer 6351?

   A   6 + 351   C   2564 + 3787

   B   6010 + 241   D   1536 + 5815

8. What are the missing digits **P** and **Q** in the problem?

$$
\begin{array}{r}
5\ 6\ \mathbf{P}\ 4 \\
+\ \mathbf{Q}\ 6\ 7\ 8 \\
\hline
8\ 3\ 1\ 2
\end{array}
$$

   A   P: 3, Q: 2   C   P: 4, Q: 2

   B   P: 3, Q: 3   D   P: 4, Q: 3

9. There were 1794 men, 825 women and 973 children at a
baseball game.
How many people were there altogether?

   A   1798   C   2767

   B   2619   D   3592

Primary Mathematics (Standards Edition) Tests 3A   © 2008 Marshall Cavendish International (Singapore) Private Lt[d]

. Susan did the following estimation to check the answer to an addition problem.

$$
\begin{array}{r}
3\,0\,0\,0 \\
+\ 6\,0\,0\,0 \\
\hline
9\,0\,0\,0
\end{array}
$$

Which of the following problems was she estimating?

A   2 7 6 3
\ \ \ + 5 4 7 2
\ \ \ [\ \ \ \ \ ]

C   2 4 9 8
\ \ \ + 6 8 7 3
\ \ \ [\ \ \ \ \ ]

B   2 8 6 5
\ \ \ + 6 1 7 8
\ \ \ [\ \ \ \ \ ]

D   3 6 1 2
\ \ \ + 6 7 5 9
\ \ \ [\ \ \ \ \ ]

Blank

Unit 2: Addition and Subtraction

Chapter 6: Subtracting Ones, Tens, Hundreds and Thousands

Subtract 9 from 5140. _____

What is 20 less than 3617? _____

There were 3425 tickets to a game.
After some tickets were sold, 700 tickets were left.
How many tickets were sold?

_____ tickets were sold.

Write the missing digit in the box.

```
    7 □ 9 6
  −   8 4 3
    6 4 5 3
```

5. Use addition to check if the following is correct.

$$\begin{array}{r} 4\,6\,0\,0 \\ -\ 1\,3\,5\,4 \\ \hline 3\,2\,4\,6 \end{array}$$

Estimation

Is the subtraction correct? _____

6. Subtract 2536 from 7419. _____

7. Round 9005 and 4316 to the nearest thousand to check if the difference is reasonable.

Estimation

$9005 - 4316 = 4689$

Is the answer reasonable? _____

8. There are 3749 yellow lights and 4256 blue lights on a Christmas tree.
How many more blue lights than yellow lights are there?

There are _____ more blue lights than yellow lights.

Primary Mathematics (Standards Edition) Tests 3A   © 2008 Marshall Cavendish International (Singapore) Private Li

Esther earns $5000.
She earns $1995 more than Shirley.
How much does Shirley earn?

Shirley earns $_____.

. Write the missing digit in each box.

$$\begin{array}{r} \boxed{}\,5\ 2\ 4 \\ -\ 3\ 7\ \boxed{}\ 6 \\ \hline 7\ 2\ 8 \end{array}$$

. Jim rounded two numbers to check if their difference was reasonable.

6000 − 2000 = 4000

What were the two numbers he rounded?

| 5299 | 1832 | 2515 | 6700 | 5713 | 1396 |

Write the two numbers in the boxes below and find their difference.

$$\begin{array}{r} \boxed{} \\ -\ \boxed{} \\ \hline \boxed{} \end{array}$$

12. There are 978 pages in Dictionary A.
    There are 1485 pages in Dictionary B.
    There are 2312 pages in Dictionary C.

    (a) How many fewer pages are there in Dictionary B tha
        in Dictionary C?

        There are _____ fewer pages in Dictionary B.

    (b) How many more pages are there in Dictionary B tha
        in Dictionary A?

        There are _____ more pages in Dictionary B.

Primary Mathematics (Standards Edition) Tests 3A   © 2008 Marshall Cavendish International (Singapore) Private L

Test B **Unit 2:** Addition and Subtraction

Chapter 6: Subtracting Ones, Tens, Hundreds and Thousands

Circle the correct option, **A**, **B**, **C** or **D**.

Subtract 5 from 7653.

A	2653	**C**	7603
B	7153	**D**	7648

The children from School P cut 2570 paper hearts for a charity.
The children from School Q cut 90 fewer paper hearts.
How many hearts did the children from School Q cut?

A	2480	**C**	2660
B	2520	**D**	7570

5765 − 3972 = 1793
Round 5765 and 3972 to the nearest thousand to check if the difference is reasonable.

A	5000 − 3000	**C**	6000 − 3000
B	5000 − 4000	**D**	6000 − 4000

What is 3071 less than 6304?

A	3233	**C**	3373
B	3303	**D**	9375

©8 Marshall Cavendish International (Singapore) Private Limited

Primary Mathematics (Standards Edition) Tests 3A

5. What is 5742 − 2785?

    A   2957   **C**   3057

    B   3043   **D**   8527

6. Which would you use to check if the answer to the following problem is correct?

$$\begin{array}{r} 4\,5\,2\,6 \\ -\ 3\,6\,8\,7 \\ \hline 8\,3\,9 \end{array}$$

    A   3687 + 839   **C**   4526 + 3687

    B   4526 + 839   **D**   4500 + 800

7. What are the missing digits **P** and **Q** in the problem below?

$$\begin{array}{r} P\,3\,6\,5 \\ -\ 2\,7\,8\,6 \\ \hline 6\,5\,7\,Q \end{array}$$

    A   P: 4, Q: 1   **C**   P: 9, Q: 9

    B   P: 8, Q: 9   **D**   P: 9, Q: 4

8. Subtract 7625 from 10,000.

    A   1375   **C**   3625

    B   2375   **D**   17,625

Primary Mathematics (Standards Edition) Tests 3A

© 2008 Marshall Cavendish International (Singapore) Private Lir

Malik saved $6174 and Betty saved $2987.
How much less than Malik did Betty save?

A $3187   C $4813

B $4787   D $9761

0. Philip did the following estimation to check if the difference
between two numbers was reasonable.

7000 − 4000 = 3000

Which of the following problems was he checking?

A   6502 − 4756   C   6825 − 3412

B   7149 − 4462   D   7512 − 3856

8 Marshall Cavendish International (Singapore) Private Limited

Blank

Test A

Unit 2: Addition and Subtraction

Chapter 7: Two-step Word Problems

Carla has 92 beads.
18 of the beads are red, 25 are green and the rest are yellow.
How many yellow beads are there?

There are _____ yellow beads.

Faizal saved $500 in April.
In May, he saved $326 more than in April.
In June, he saved $187 more than in May.
How much did he save altogether?

He saved $_____ altogether.

©8 Marshall Cavendish International (Singapore) Private Limited
Primary Mathematics (Standards Edition) Tests 3A

3. There were 1120 women at a basketball game.
   There were 245 more men than women.
   There were 718 fewer children than men.
   How many children were there?

   There were _____ children.

4. Mary earns $4785.
   She spends $1548 on transport and $2850 on food.
   How much does she have left?

   She has $_____ left.

There are 3517 members in a club.
1825 are men, 725 are children and the rest are women.
How many women are there?

There are _____ women.

Look at the number of buttons sewn on by two machines.

Machine A	1549
Machine B	1826

(a)   Which machine sewed on more buttons?
How many more?

Machine _____ sewed on _____ more buttons.

(b)   How many buttons did the two machines sew on
altogether?

The machines sewed on _____ buttons altogether.

7. Look at the solution to a word problem below.

Word Problem

Alfred had $7193.
He gave $1927 to his mother and spent $2803.
How much did he have left?

Solution

7193 − 1927 = 5266
He had $5266 left after giving $1927 to his mother.

5266 − 2803 = 2463
He had $2463 left.

Round all the numbers, except for the final answer, to the nearest thousand to check if the answer is reasonable.

Is the answer reasonable? _____

Primary Mathematics (Standards Edition) Tests 3A   © 2008 Marshall Cavendish International (Singapore) Private Li

Mr. Chan earned $5730 in January, spent some money and had $2487 left.
In February, he earned $5900 and spent all of it.
How much did he spend altogether?

He spent $_____ altogether.

Ben and Susie used their cellphones to send and receive messages.
Their bill showed a total of 3647 messages.
1853 of the messages were Ben's.

(a) How many messages were Susie's?

_____ messages were Susie's.

(b) Who had more messages? How many more?

_____ had _____ more messages.

10. Polly played a game and scored 2376 points.
    She scored 1520 more points than Kenneth.
    How many points did they score altogether?

They scored _____ points altogether.

Test B

Unit 2: Addition and Subtraction

Chapter 7: Two-step Word Problems

Circle the correct option, **A**, **B**, **C** or **D**.

Jim had **64** stickers.
Marla gave him **17** stickers and in turn Jim gave her
21 stickers.
How many stickers did Jim have left?

A   60   **C**   85

B   63   **D**   102

Hazel scored **600** more points than Peter in a game.
Peter scored **1848** points.
How many points did the two of them score altogether?

A   1248   **C**   3048

B   2448   **D**   4296

There were **1482** boys in a school.
There were **96** more boys than girls in the school.
How many students were there in the school?

A   1386   **C**   2868

B   1578   **D**   3060

4. Darren saved $2156.
His sister saved $234 less than he did.
His brother saved $409 less than his sister did.
How much did Darren's brother save?

   A $1513   C $2331

   B $1981   D $2799

5. The table shows the number of toys made in three factorie
A total of 10,000 toys were made.

Factory P	3085
Factory Q	5462
Factory R	?

How many toys were made in Factory R?

   A   1453   C   6915

   B   4538   D   8547

6. Ken used a photocopier to print 2612 copies on Tuesday.
On Wednesday, he wanted to print 622 fewer copies tha
on Tuesday.
However, the machine broke down after printing 1427 copie
How many copies could he not print?

   A   563   C   1807

   B   805   D   1990

Primary Mathematics (Standards Edition) Tests 3A   © 2008 Marshall Cavendish International (Singapore) Private Li

In the first week of the month, a factory produces 5149 cans of tuna and sells all of them.
In the second week of the month, it produces 3856 cans, sells some cans and has 778 cans left.
How many cans of tuna are sold altogether in the two weeks?

A   3078   **C**   9005

B   8227   **D**   9783

Out of 3218 tickets sold, 1592 tickets were for a football game.
The rest were for a basketball game.
Complete the following sentence.
_____ more tickets were sold for the _____ game.

A   34, basketball   **C**   1626, basketball

B   34, football   **D**   1626, football

Alice bought a piano for $2148.
Betty's piano cost $632 more than Alice's piano.
Betty's piano cost $215 less than Carmen's piano.
How much did Carmen's piano cost?

A $1301   **C** $2780

B $2560   **D** $2995

Turn the page.

10. A total of 4215 people attended a book fair.
1647 people attended in the morning.
How many more people attended in the afternoon?
Which of the following shows the correct steps?

A   4215 − 1647 = 2568
2568 − 1647 = 921

B   4215 − 1647 = 2568
2568 + 1647 = 4215

C   4215 + 1647 = 5862
5862 − 1647 = 4215

D   4215 + 1647 = 5862
5862 + 1647 = 7509

Units 1–2

Write the number in words.

5036

_____

What does the digit 5 in 5782 stand for? _____

Arrange the numbers in order.
Begin with the greatest.

3519, 865, 7215, 3579

_____

Complete the regular number pattern.

3479, 3379, _____, 3179, _____

Fill in each ◯ with **>**, **<** or **=**.

(a) 37 – 17 ◯ 10 + 7

(b) 21 + 45 ◯ 85 – 37

© Marshall Cavendish International (Singapore) Private Limited

6. Round 8725 to the nearest thousand. _____

7. What number is 8 more than 326? _____

8. Find the sum of 35 and 96. _____

9. Find the difference between 76 and 7526. _____

10. What number is 968 less than 4521?_____

11. _____ − 89 = 1386

12. Write the missing number in the box.

    71 − 26 = 18 + ☐

13. Subtract 5274 from 10,000.
    Show your working below.

14. Add 1349 to 3786.
    Show your working below.

Primary Mathematics (Standards Edition) Tests 3A   © 2008 Marshall Cavendish International (Singapore) Private Li

5. At a carnival, 3412 tokens were sold.
2678 of the tokens were sold for $1 each and the rest for
$2 each.
How many $2 tokens were sold?

_____ $2 tokens were sold.

6. There were 8542 men at a game.
There were 918 more men than women.
How many women were there?

There were _____ women.

7. A baker baked 6735 loaves of bread.
1857 loaves were banana walnut bread, 2051 loaves were
raisin bread and the rest of the loaves were plain bread.
How many loaves of plain bread were there?

There were _____ loaves of plain bread.

08 Marshall Cavendish International (Singapore) Private Limited

18. Mr. Lee spent $2589 on food and $673 less on transport.
    He saved $125 less than the amount he spent on transpor
    How much did he save?

    He saved $_____.

19. Three machines printed the number of calendars shown belov

Machine A	1786
Machine B	3152
Machine C	?

    Machine C printed the total number of calendars printed
    by both Machine A and Machine B.
    How many calendars did the machines print altogether?

    The machines printed _____ calendars altogether.

Primary Mathematics (Standards Edition) Tests 3A   © 2008 Marshall Cavendish International (Singapore) Private Li

Cumulative Test B **Units 1–2**

Circle the correct option, **A**, **B**, **C** or **D**.

Which shows six thousand, two hundred eight in standard form?

A   628   **C**   6280

B   6208   **D**   8206

A factory makes 1398 pens.
Which of the following is equal to 1398?

A   1 + 3 + 9 + 8   **C**   1000 + 300 + 90 + 8

B   1 + 300 + 90 + 8   **D**   8000 + 900 + 300 + 1

Which number has the digit 3 in the hundreds place?

A   1538   **C**   3521

B   2356   **D**   8423

Which number is **greater** than 362 but **smaller** than 584?

A   592   **C**   359

B   398   **D**   222

Which number is 100 more than 6372?

A   6273   **C**   6382

B   6362   **D**   6472

©08 Marshall Cavendish International (Singapore) Private Limited   Primary Mathematics (Standards Edition) Tests 3A

6. Which of the following is the smallest number that becomes 340 when rounded to the nearest ten?

   A 349   **C** 335

   B 341   **D** 331

7. Which number is 7 less than 812?

   A 742   **C** 819

   B 805   **D** 882

8. Find the sum of 19 and 895.

   A 804   **C** 914

   B 876   **D** 1085

9. What is the difference between 257 and 1038?

   A 781   **C** 1295

   B 1221   **D** 3208

10. Which number belongs in the box?

    $281 + \boxed{} = 300$

    A 19   **C** 519

    B 181   **D** 581

11. Which sign belongs in the $\bigcirc$?

    $172 + 839 \bigcirc 2005 - 896$

    A >   **C** <

    B =   **D** +

Primary Mathematics (Standards Edition) Tests 3A

2. Subtract 2934 from 6107.

   A   3173   **C**   8031

   B   4833   **D**   9041

3. 5329 + 2879 = _____

   A   2450   **C**   7198

   B   3550   **D**   8208

4. Which sign belongs in each $\bigcirc$?

   317 $\bigcirc$ 634 $\bigcirc$ 785 − 295

   A   +, <   **C**   −, <

   B   +, >   **D**   −, >

5. To decorate the school, Class P made **862** paper streamers and Class Q made **1000** paper streamers.
How many more paper streamers did Class Q make?

   A   138   **C**   1862

   B   262   **D**   9620

6. 5163 cellphones were made by a factory in two days.

Day 1	3562
Day 2	?

How many cellphones were made on the second day?

   A   1601   **C**   8625

   B   2401   **D**   8725

17. Stanley saved $3512 last year.
He has saved $1269 more this year.
How much has he saved in the two years?

A	$2243	**C**	$7283
B	$4781	**D**	$8293

18. There were 6094 people at a concert.
There were 2784 children, 1386 women and some men.
How many men were there?

A	1924	**C**	4170
B	3310	**D**	4708

19. Mili scored 2749 points at a game.
She scored 987 more points than Cindy.
Pete scored 156 fewer points than Cindy.
How many points did Pete score?

A	1606	**C**	3736
B	3508	**D**	3892

20. The table shows the number of pencils produced by three machines.

Machine A	Machine B	Machine C
1786	2348	?

639 fewer pencils were produced by Machine C than by Machine A.
How many pencils were produced by the three machines in al

A	1709	**C**	4134
B	4057	**D**	5281

Primary Mathematics (Standards Edition) Tests 3A

Test A

Unit 3: Multiplication and Division

Chapter 1: Looking Back

How many candles are there in the picture below?
Show your answer in multiplication and repeated
addition forms.

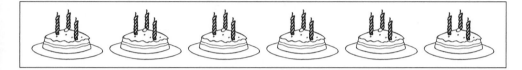

_____ × _____ = _____

_____ + _____ + _____ + _____ + _____ + _____ = _____

Alan bought 6 books.
If each book cost $4, how much did he pay?

6 × $_____ = $_____

He paid $ _____.

Show your answer in repeated addition form.

_____

©8 Marshall Cavendish International (Singapore) Private Limited   Primary Mathematics (Standards Edition) Tests 3A

3. How many wheels do 5 cars have?
Fill in each blank with the missing number.

Number of cars	1	2	3	4	5
Number of wheels	4	8	12	16	?

5 × 4 = _____

5 cars have _____ wheels.

4. How many stars are there?
Fill in each blank with the missing number.

_____ × _____ = _____

5. There were some dogs.
Mary counted 28 legs altogether.
How many dogs were there?

There were _____ dogs.

6. Janet bought 8 bracelets, each costing $10.

She paid $_____ altogether.

Primary Mathematics (Standards Edition) Tests 3A   © 2008 Marshall Cavendish International (Singapore) Private Li

Write two multiplication sentences for the picture below.

_____ × _____ = _____

_____ × _____ = _____

There are _____ flowers.

There are 30 buttons on 10 shirts.

How many buttons are there on each shirt?

30 ÷ 10 = _____

There are _____ buttons on each shirt.

Fill in each blank with the missing number.

(a)   10 × _____ = 0

(b)   _____ × 7 = 7

. Fill in each blank with the missing number.

_____ × 4 = 20

20 ÷ 4 = _____

11. Fill in each ◯ with **+, –, ÷** or **×**.

(a) 4 ◯ 3 = 12

(b) 24 ◯ 8 = 16

(c) 25 ◯ 5 = 5

(d) 12 ◯ 6 = 18

12. Mawan threw seven darts in a game as shown below.
Each dart that hit the center ring of the dartboard was worth 3 points.
Each dart that hit the other rings was not worth any points.
How many points did Mawan score?

_____ × _____ = _____

He scored _____ points.

Primary Mathematics (Standards Edition) Tests 3A

© 2008 Marshall Cavendish International (Singapore) Private L

Test B

Unit 3: Multiplication and Division

Chapter 1: Looking Back

Circle the correct option, **A**, **B**, **C** or **D**.

A ball cost $3.
Tony bought 5 balls.
How much did he pay?

Number of balls	1	2	3	4	5
Cost of balls	$3	$6	$9	$12	?

A $2   **C** $15

B $8   **D** $18

How many oranges are there?

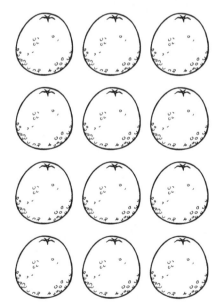

A 3 + 3   **C** 4 + 4 + 4

B 3 + 3 + 3   **D** 4 + 4 + 4 + 4

Primary Mathematics (Standards Edition) Tests 3A

3. Which sign belongs in the ◯?

   4 ◯ 7 = 28

   A +   **C** ×

   B −   **D** ÷

4. How many pencils are there?

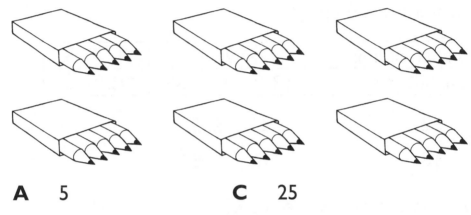

   A 5   **C** 25

   B 6   **D** 30

5. How many circles are there?

   A 1 × 3   **C** 3 × 3

   B 2 × 3   **D** 4 × 3

6. What is the missing number in the box?

   ☐ × 5 = 0

   A 0   **C** 5

   B 1   **D** 10

How many dimes are there in $6?

A   1   **C**   10

B   6   **D**   60

Which number belongs in the boxes?

8 × ☐ = 40

40 ÷ ☐ = 8

A   5   **C**   32

B   10   **D**   48

Which division sentence is modeled by the following figure?

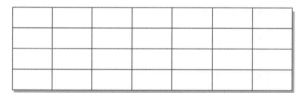

A   12 ÷ 3 = 4   **C**   28 ÷ 4 = 7

B   40 ÷ 10 = 4   **D**   21 ÷ 3 = 7

. Complete the number sentence.

10 ◯ 2 = ☐

A (+), 5   **C** (−), 5

B (×), 2   **D** (÷), 5

8 Marshall Cavendish International (Singapore) Private Limited   Primary Mathematics (Standards Edition) Tests 3A

11. Which sign belongs in the ( )?

   3×6 ( ) 2×9

   A >   C <

   B =   D ÷

12. Shelby buys 9 apples every week.
    How many apples does she buy in 4 weeks?

   A 27   C 45

   B 36   D 49

13. Betty used 45 beads to make necklaces.
    She used 5 beads for each necklace.
    How many necklaces did she make?

   A 9   C 50

   B 40   D 225

14. Dennis received a sticker for every 3 words spelled corre
    If he received 7 stickers, how many words did he spell
    correctly?

   A $7 + 3$ C 7×3

   B $7 - 3$ D $7 \div 3$

15. The milkman delivers 27 bottles of milk to 9 houses every da
    Each house gets the same number of bottles.
    How many bottles of milk does each house get?

   A 3   C 12

   B 6   D 36

Primary Mathematics (Standards Edition) Tests 3A

© 2008 Marshall Cavendish International (Singapore) Private Li

20

Test A | **Unit 3:** Multiplication and Division
Chapter 2: More Word Problems

There are 7 packets of tissues.
There are 10 tissues in each packet.
How many tissues are there altogether?

There are _____ tissues.

27 cards were shared equally among 3 boys.
How many cards did each boy get?

Each boy got _____ cards.

Eddie fixes a total of 24 wheels onto some toy cars.
How many toy cars are there?

There are _____ toy cars.

4. Mrs. Cruz bought some pens and divided them equally among 5 students.
Each student received 3 pens.
How many pens did Mrs. Cruz buy?

She bought _____ pens.

5. 5 friends shared the cost of a meal equally.
Each person paid $7.
What was the total cost of the meal?

The total cost of the meal was $_____.

6. Tom and Hardy scored 9 points each.
Sam scored 12 points.
How many points did the boys score altogether?

They scored _____ points altogether.

Primary Mathematics (Standards Edition) Tests 3A
© 2008 Marshall Cavendish International (Singapore) Private Li

Mavis had $100 in the bank.
She wanted to use an equal amount each day for 10 days.

(a) How much could she use each day?

She could use $_____ each day.

(b) She took out the amount of money she could use in a day and spent $7 of it.
How much did she have left for the day?

She had $_____ left.

In a class, there are 8 boys.
There are 3 times as many girls as boys.
How many more girls than boys are there?

There are _____ more girls.

8 Marshall Cavendish International (Singapore) Private Limited

Primary Mathematics (Standards Edition) Tests 3A

9. There are 20 green chairs in a room.
   There are 4 times as many green chairs as yellow chairs.
   Lara puts in 7 more yellow chairs.
   How many yellow chairs are there now?

   There are _____ yellow chairs now.

10. Amy has $2.
    Balu has 3 times as much as Amy.
    Catherine has twice as much as Balu.
    How much does Catherine have?

    Catherine has $_____.

Primary Mathematics (Standards Edition) Tests 3A

. Mrs. Lee used 6 m of material to sew 3 dresses.
She used 4 times as much material for a curtain as for a dress.
How much material did she use for the curtain?

She used _____ of material for the curtain.

. Bag A weighs 15 kg.
Bag B weighs 3 kg.
Bag C is twice the weight of both Bag A and Bag B.
How much does Bag C weigh?

Bag C weighs _____.

13. Farah read 42 books.
    Harry read 12 fewer books than Farah.
    Harry read 3 times as many books than Max.
    How many books did Max read?

    Max read _____ books.

Primary Mathematics (Standards Edition) Tests 3A

Test B

Unit 3: Multiplication and Division

Chapter 2: More Word Problems

Circle the correct option, **A**, **B**, **C** or **D**.

There are 6 goldfish in a tank.
There are 3 times as many angelfish as goldfish.
How many angelfish are there?

A   2   **C**   9

B   3   **D**   18

To make horseshoes, Patrick counted the legs of
the horses on his farm.
There were 20 legs.
How many horses were there?

A   2   **C**   10

B   5   **D**   80

Pamela worked for 9 hours.
She earned $3 an hour.
Which is the correct operation to find out how much she
earned altogether?

A   3 + 9   **C**   3 × 9

B   9 − 3   **D**   9 ÷ 3

4. Lily delivered 18 copies of newspapers.
   She delivered twice as many copies as Farah.
   How many copies did Farah deliver?

   A   9   **C**   20

   B   16   **D**   36

5. Bill bought 12 pencils.
   He bought 3 times as many pencils as pens.
   He bought 2 more erasers than pens.
   How many erasers did he buy?

   A   2   **C**   12

   B   6   **D**   17

6. 40 gallons of water is poured into a container.
   There is 4 times as much water in the container as in a tank.
   Ben removes 3 gallons of water from the tank.
   How much water is there in the tank now?

   A   3 gallons   **C**   33 gallons

   B   7 gallons   **D**   47 gallons

7. There were 26 boys at a camp.
   There were 2 fewer girls than boys.
   4 girls slept in each tent.
   How many tents were needed for the girls?

   A   6   **C**   24

   B   8   **D**   96

Primary Mathematics (Standards Edition) Tests 3A   © 2008 Marshall Cavendish International (Singapore) Private Lim

Mrs. Kelly made 16 corn biscuits.
She made 4 more almond biscuits than corn biscuits.
10 boys shared the almond biscuits equally.
How many almond biscuits did each boy eat?

A   1   **C**   20

B   2   **D**   30

A rod is 7 in. long.
There are 5 rods.
They are all cut from a piece of wood 42 in. long.
How many inches of wood is left?

A   6 in.   **C**   11 in.

B   7 in.   **D**   35 in.

. Anthony has 12 postcards.
He has 3 times as many postcards as Belle.
Mabel has half as many postcards as Belle.
How many postcards does Mabel have?

A   2   **C**   8

B   4   **D**   16

8 Marshall Cavendish International (Singapore) Private Limited   Primary Mathematics (Standards Edition) Tests 3A

Blank

Test A **Unit 3:** Multiplication and Division

Chapter 3: Multiplying Ones, Tens, Hundreds and Thousands

Multiply 36 by 3.

_____

There are 24 hours in a day.
How many hours are there in 4 days?

_____

8 students made 215 paper cranes each.
How many paper cranes did they make in all?

_____

What is 645 × 0?

_____

Find the product of 3192 and 2.

_____

6. Esther did the following multiplication problem.

$$\begin{array}{r} 1\,8\,9\,8 \\ \times \quad\quad 3 \\ \hline 5\,6\,9\,4 \end{array}$$

Round **1898** to the nearest thousand to check if the answw
is reasonable.

Estimation

Is the answer reasonable? _____

7. There are **4735** sheets of paper in one stack.
How many sheets of paper are there in **2** such stacks?

There are _____ sheets of paper in 2 stacks.

8. Sam saves $12 every day.
Wally saves $7 more than Sam every day.
How much does Wally save in 5 days?

Wally saves $_____ in 5 days.

Primary Mathematics (Standards Edition) Tests 3A
© 2008 Marshall Cavendish International (Singapore) Private Lin

Alison and Bernard work in a bakery.
Alison makes 135 buns in a day.
Bernard makes 18 fewer buns than Alison in a day.
How many buns does Bernard make in 3 days?

He makes _____ buns in 3 days.

. Mrs. Lynn sold 748 books in the first week of a book sale.
In the second week, she sold 4 times as many books.
In the third week, she sold 897 fewer books than in the
second week.
How many books did she sell in the third week?

She sold _____ books in the third week.

11. Kimberly bought 542 beads.
    She bought 157 fewer beads than Alice.
    Alice bought the same number of beads for 3 days.
    How many beads did Alice buy altogether?

    She bought _____ beads altogether.

Test B

Unit 3: Multiplication and Division

Chapter 3: Multiplying Ones, Tens, Hundreds and Thousands

Circle the correct option, **A**, **B**, **C** or **D**.

What is the product of 70 and 5?

A	35	**C**	350
B	75	**D**	750

Which number belongs in the box?

☐ × 5 = 4500

A	9	**C**	900
B	90	**D**	9000

There are 200 sheep on a farm.
How many legs do the sheep have altogether?

A	40	**C**	400
B	80	**D**	800

Mr. Yamada saved $78 every week for 2 weeks.
How much did he save altogether?

A	$39	**C**	$80
B	$76	**D**	$156

Multiply 167 by 5.

A	162	**C**	835
B	172	**D**	880

8 Marshall Cavendish International (Singapore) Private Limited

6. Which sign belongs in the $\bigcirc$?

   425 $\bigcirc$ 5 = 2125

   A   +   C   ×
   B   ÷   D   −

7. Estimate the product of 578 and 3.

   A   500 × 3   C   600 × 3
   B   500 × 4   D   600 × 4

8. Lemy deposits $2135 of his salary into the bank every month.
   How much does he deposit into the bank after 4 months?

   A $2131   C $4270
   B $2139   D $8540

9. There were 850 adults at a game.
   There were 3 times as many teenagers as adults.
   How many people were there at the game?

   A   853   C   2550
   B   1700   D   3400

10. Xavier has $36 more than Cindy.
    Mandy has twice as much as Cindy.
    If Xavier has $915, how much does Mandy have?

    A $879   C $1758
    B $951   D $1830

Test A

Unit 3: Multiplication and Division

Chapter 4: Quotient and Remainder

There are 17 stars below.
Put an equal number into each of the 4 ovals.

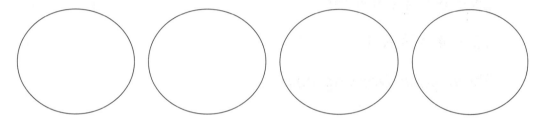

(a) How many stars are there in each oval? _____

(b) How many stars are left? _____

Divide 7 by 2.

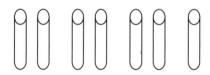

Quotient = _____   Remainder = _____

3. Is there a remainder when you divide 18 by 3? _____
   Show your working below.

4. How would you check if the answer to the following
   problem is correct?

   13 ÷ 4 = 3 R 1

   Show your working below.

Mary has 16 beads.
She uses 5 beads to make a necklace.
How many necklaces can she make?

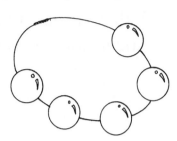

She can make _____ necklaces.

The following shows how Gerald checked a division problem.

$2 \times 9 = 18$
$18 + 1 = 19$

What was the division problem he was checking?
Fill in each blank with the missing number.

_____ ÷ _____ = _____

There are 26 pretzels.
Mrs. Green puts them equally into 3 jars.
She gives the remainder to Brandon.
How many pretzels does Brandon get?

Brandon gets _____ pretzels.

8 Marshall Cavendish International (Singapore) Private Limited

8. I want to divide a number by 4 and have a remainder of ⁝
   The number is greater than 10 and smaller than 20.
   What is the **greatest** possible number?
   Show your working below.

   The greatest possible number is _____.

9. Divide 40 by 3.

   $$3\overline{)40}$$

   The quotient is _____.

   The remainder is _____.

0. How would you check if the answer for the following division problem is correct?

$$\begin{array}{r} 2\ 3 \\ 4\overline{)9\ 5} \\ \underline{8} \\ 1\ 5 \\ \underline{1\ 2} \\ 3 \end{array}$$

$$95 \div 4 = 23 \text{ R } 3$$

Show your working below.

. Marinda has 85 ft of material.
She uses 10 ft to make one curtain panel.

(a) How many curtain panels can she make?

She can make _____ curtain panels.

(b) How much material will she have left?

She will have _____ ft of material left.

12. Edmund was paid $78 for 4 days.
    He was given an equal amount for each day of work and an extra $2 for doing a good job.
    How much was he paid a day?

    He was paid $_____ a day.

13. Fill in the box with **T** if the statement is true, or **F** if the statement is false.

    (a) For 45 ÷ 4, the remainder is an odd number. ☐

    (b) 74 ÷ 4 = 18 + 2 ☐

    (c) When 60 is divided by 5, the quotient is 12. ☐

Primary Mathematics (Standards Edition) Tests 3A

© 2008 Marshall Cavendish International (Singapore) Private Lim

Test
B

Unit 3: Multiplication and Division

Chapter 4: Quotient and Remainder

Circle the correct option, **A**, **B**, **C** or **D**.

What is the quotient when you divide 98 by 5?

98 ÷ 5 = 19 R 3

A 3   **C** 19

B 11   **D** 20

Divide 16 by 3.

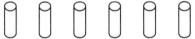

A 1 R 5   **C** 5 R 1

B 2 R 1   **D** 6 R 1

25 students got into groups of 4.
How many students were left after the groups were formed?

A 1   **C** 3

B 2   **D** 6

There are 37 people.
All of them have to go to a party.
If a cab can take 4 people, how many cabs are needed for
all of them?

A 3   **C** 9

B 4   **D** 10

5. How would you check if the following answer is correct?

$17 \div 2 = 8 \text{ R } 1$

A $1 \times 17 = 17$

C $8 \times 2 = 16$
$16 + 1 = 17$

B $4 \times 4 = 16$
$16 + 1 = 17$

D $9 \times 2 = 18$
$18 - 1 = 17$

6. Which of the following will **not** have a remainder?

A $12 \div 5$

C $21 \div 3$

B $14 \div 3$

D $33 \div 4$

7. Divide 47 by 3.

A   12 R 1

C   15 R 2

B   15

D   50

8. What is $84 \div 7$?

A   9

C   77

B   12

D   91

9. Complete the number sentence.

$35 \div 5 = \boxed{\text{P}} + \boxed{\text{Q}}$

A   P: 5, Q: 2

C   P: 7, Q: 5

B   P: 7, Q: 2

D   P: 30, Q: 5

Primary Mathematics (Standards Edition) Tests 3A   © 2008 Marshall Cavendish International (Singapore) Private Lim

. Cindy saved an equal number of dimes over 5 days.
If she saved $4 in dimes, how many dimes did she save
each day?

A 4   **C** 8

B 5   **D** 10

. There were 99 people at a restaurant.
4 people were seated at each table.
The remaining people sat at the last table.
How many people sat at the last table?

A 3   **C** 24

B 4   **D** 25

. Which number will have a remainder of 1 when divided by 3?

A 50   **C** 70

B 60   **D** 80

. There are 62 toys.
A shopkeeper displays 5 toys on each shelf and keeps the
remaining toys.
How many shelves are needed and how many toys does
she keep?

A   6 shelves; 2 toys kept

B   12 shelves; 0 toys kept

C   12 shelves; 2 toys kept

D   102 shelves; 2 toys kept

14. Betty decorates each table with a vase of flowers. If she puts 3 flowers in each vase, how many tables can she decorate with 76 flowers?

   A 25   **C** 79

   B 73   **D** 228

15. An even number is divided by 4.
    It has a quotient of 11 and a remainder of 2.
    What is the number?

   A 22   **C** 46

   B 44   **D** 52

Primary Mathematics (Standards Edition) Tests 3A

Unit 3: Multiplication and Division

Chapter 5: Dividing Hundreds, Tens and Ones

$600 \div 2 =$ _____

Divide.

$$2\overline{)3\ 7\ 0}$$

Ross did the problem below.

$730 \div 5 = 146$

Show how you would check his answer using multiplication.

```
┌─────────────────────┐
│ Estimation          │
│                     │
│                     │
│                     │
│                     │
│                     │
│                     │
│                     │
└─────────────────────┘
```

Is the quotient correct? _____

4. Divide 173 by 4.

Quotient = _____

Remainder = _____

5. What is the quotient when 152 is divided by 5?

The quotient is _____.

612 people signed up for a course.
They were put into 3 rooms.
How many people were there in each room?

There were _____ people in each room.

A fruit seller puts 10 oranges in a box.
There are 318 oranges.
How many boxes are needed if all of the oranges have to
be put into boxes?

_____ boxes are needed.

8. Karen strings some beads to make necklaces.
   She strings 149 beads a day for 4 days.
   She then has 3 beads left to string.
   How many beads does she have altogether?

   The following is what Tim did to find the answer.

   <u>Solution</u>

   149 × 4 = 596   1 4 9
   596 + 3 = 599   ×   4
                        —————
                        5 9 6

   She has 599 beads altogether.

   How would you check if Tim's answer is correct?
   Show your working below.

Primary Mathematics (Standards Edition) Tests 3A   © 2008 Marshall Cavendish International (Singapore) Private Li

Josephine made 640 pints of juice for a big party.
She poured 3 pints of juice into each glass.
How many glasses were filled and how much juice was left over?

_____ glasses were filled.

_____ of juice was left over.

9. 738 cookies were put into 5 boxes.
How many more cookies are needed so that there will be an equal number of cookies in each box?

_____ more cookies are needed.

11. There were 257 boys in a school.
    There were 67 more girls than boys.
    The girls were put into groups of 4.
    How many groups of girls were there?

    There were _____ groups of girls.

12. Susie has $716.
    She has $18 more than Ben.
    Ben has twice as much as Gayle.
    How much does Gayle have?

    Gayle has $_____.

Primary Mathematics (Standards Edition) Tests 3A

Test B

Unit 3: Multiplication and Division

Chapter 5: Dividing Hundreds, Tens and Ones

Circle the correct option, **A**, **B**, **C** or **D**.

Divide 800 by 2.

A 4

C 400

B 40

D 802

$100 \div 3 =$ _____

A 13 R 3

C 33 R 1

B 30 R 1

D 330 R 1

What is the remainder when 187 is divided by 5?

A 1

C 3

B 2

D 4

What is the quotient when 506 is divided by 3?

A 2

C 168

B 16

D 169

Which number will give 100 when divided by 10?

A 10

C 1000

B 100

D 10,000

6. Which of the following can be used to check if the answer below is correct?

   $300 \div 4 = 75$

   A $75 \times 4 = 300$ **C** $150 \times 2 = 300$

   B $100 \times 3 = 300$ **D** $300 - 75 - 75 = 150$

7. $417 \div 4 =$ _____

   A 14 R 1   **C** 100 R 17

   B 14 R 3   **D** 104 R 1

8. Brian had 625 stamps.
   He put 10 stamps on each page of his album and put the remainder on the last page.
   How many pages of stamps did he have?

   A 60   **C** 62

   B 61   **D** 63

9. $670 was shared equally among 5 people.
   How much did each person get?

   A $110   **C** $130 R 20

   B $114   **D** $134

10. 206 oranges and 138 apples were put equally into 4 cartor
    How many fruits were there in each carton?

    A 17   **C** 86

    B 68   **D** 344

Primary Mathematics (Standards Edition) Tests 3A

© 2008 Marshall Cavendish International (Singapore) Private Li

1. There were 127 red flags and twice as many blue flags.
   The flags were strung onto 3 strings.
   How many flags were there on each string?

   A 84   **C** 254

   B 127   **D** 381

2. At a party, 67 adults and 40 children were present.
   They sat at tables in groups of 5.
   The remaining people occupied one table.
   How many tables did all the people occupy?

   A 21   **C** 72

   B 22   **D** 117

3. Mrs. Lennox earned $4 an hour for her work.
   If she earned $740, how many hours did she work?

   A 37   **C** 185

   B 148   **D** 749

4. How many threes are there in 6 × 4?

   A 2   **C** 6

   B 4   **D** 8

Turn the page.

15. A shopkeeper packed 210 cans of tuna equally into boxes of 8.
    How many boxes did he use?
    How many cans of tuna were left over?

    A   26 boxes, 2 cans left over

    B   26 boxes, 8 cans left over

    C   27 boxes, 0 cans left over

    D   27 boxes, 6 cans left over

Primary Mathematics (Standards Edition) Tests 3A   © 2008 Marshall Cavendish International (Singapore) Private Lir

Cumulative Test A — Units 1–3

$8532 = 8000 +$ _____ $+ 30 + 2$

Write in words.

1932

_____

Fill in the ◯ with **>**, **<** or **=**.

3673 ◯ $3000 + 700 + 60 + 3$

372 boys and 196 girls took part in an art competition. How many students took part in the competition?

_____ students took part in the competition.

_____ $- 2579 = 1326$

6. The sum of two numbers is 7526.

   (a) If the greater number is 4319, what is the smaller number?

       The smaller number is _____.

   (b) What is the difference between the two numbers?

       The difference is _____.

7. Fill in the ◯ with **>**, **<** or **=**.

   8 × 5 ◯ 80 ÷ 10

8. There are 6 sheep on a farm.
   There are 3 times as many cows as sheep on the farm.
   How many animals are there altogether?

   There are _____ animals.

Primary Mathematics (Standards Edition) Tests 3A

Mr. Henderson bought 3 boxes of pencils.
There were 8 pencils in each box.
The pencils were shared equally among 4 boys.
How many pencils did each boy receive?

Each boy received _____ pencils.

). _____ × 5 = 2000

. How would you check if the following answer is correct?

944 ÷ 4 = 236

Show your working below.

Is the answer correct? _____

2. Multiply 789 by 4. _____

3. What is the remainder when 385 is divided by 4?
Show your working below.

The remainder is _____.

08 Marshall Cavendish International (Singapore) Private Limited

Primary Mathematics (Standards Edition) Tests 3A

14. 9728 × _____ = 9728

15. 725 cards are shared among 5 girls.
    How many cards does each girl receive?

    Each girl receives _____ cards.

16. There are 12 boys and 15 girls in a class.
    They are put equally into 3 groups.
    How many boys and how many girls are there in
    each group?

    There are _____ boys and _____ girls in
    each group.

Primary Mathematics (Standards Edition) Tests 3A   © 2008 Marshall Cavendish International (Singapore) Private Lim

7. How would you check if the following answer is correct?

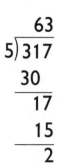

Show your working below.

Is the answer correct? _____

8. James has 430 apples.
He packs them into 4 crates.
How many apples are there in each crate?
How many apples are left?

There are _____ apples in each crate.

_____ apples are left.

19. Sam has 63 stamps.
    He has 28 more stamps than John.
    Ken has 3 times as many stamps as John.
    How many stamps does Ken have?

    Ken has _____ stamps.

20. Amy has $730.
    She has twice as much as Mandy.
    Mandy has $77 more than Suresh.
    How much does Suresh have?

    Suresh has $_____.

Cumulative Test B **Units 1–3**

Circle the correct option, **A**, **B**, **C** or **D**.

Six thousand, eight is _____.

A   68   **C**   6008

B   608   **D**   6800

What is the missing number?

$6749 -$ _____ $= 6709$

A   4   **C**   49

B   40   **D**   400

Which sign belongs in the $\bigcirc$?

$25 \;\bigcirc\; 5 = 5$

A $+$ **C** $\times$

B $-$ **D** $\div$

Which set of numbers is arranged in increasing order?

A   412, 800, 1256, 1265   **C**   1743, 1247, 1000, 743

B   1743, 978, 2035, 5178   **D**   3615, 4900, 6218, 5999

There are 927 girls in a school of 2173 students.
How many boys are there?

A   1246   **C**   7097

B   3100   **D**   10,000

6. John had 319 cards.
   He collected some more cards.
   He then had 400 cards.
   How many more cards did he collect?

   A   19   **C**   119

   B   81   **D**   719

7. Which number belongs in the boxes?

   $42 \div \boxed{} = 6$

   $\boxed{} \times 6 = 42$

   A   7   **C**   36

   B   10   **D**   48

8. What is the quotient when 17 is divided by 3?

   A   2   **C**   14

   B   5   **D**   51

9. Lily has 412 ft of material.
   She uses 10 ft to sew a dress.
   How many dresses can she sew and how much material
   will she have left?

   A   4 dresses; 12 ft of material left

   B   40 dresses; 2 ft of material left

   C   41 dresses; 2 ft of material left

   D   410 dresses; 2 ft of material left

Primary Mathematics (Standards Edition) Tests 3A   © 2008 Marshall Cavendish International (Singapore) Private Lir

. Julia has $120.
   She has 3 times as much as Chandra.
   How much does Chandra have?

   A $4   **C** $360

   B $40   **D** $400

. Ship A carried 94 containers.
   Ship B carried 15 fewer containers than Ship A.
   When the ships docked, all the containers were loaded
   and an equal number of containers were put into 4 rooms.
   How many containers were left over?

   A   1   **C**   19

   B   3   **D**   27

. There are 254 oranges at a store.
   There are twice as many apples as oranges.
   How many fruits are there altogether?

   A   127   **C**   508

   B   318   **D**   762

. There are 5 boxes of equal weight.
   They weigh 105 kg.
   What is the weight of 3 such boxes?

   A   21 kg   **C**   63 kg

   B   35 kg   **D**   113 kg

14. There are 576 red beads and 49 more blue beads than red beads.
    The beads are used to make 10 necklaces.
    Each necklace has an equal number of beads.
    How many beads are left over?

    A   1   **C**   62

    B   25   **D**   600

15. There were 785 boys in a school of 1684 students.
    Each girl in the school made 3 hair bands for a project.
    How many hair bands did they make in all?

    A   299   **C**   899

    B   823   **D**   2697

16. There were 4785 concert tickets.
    389 sets of 10 tickets each were sold.
    How many tickets were not sold?

    A   895   **C**   4396

    B   4386   **D**   5184

17. Polly has a collection of 477 pink and blue buttons.
    There are 149 more pink buttons than blue buttons.
    How many blue buttons are there?

    A   164   **C**   328

    B   313   **D**   626

Primary Mathematics (Standards Edition) Tests 3A   © 2008 Marshall Cavendish International (Singapore) Private Li

3. Julie made 30 cheese buns and 3 times as many custard buns.
How many buns did she make altogether?

A   30

B   90

C   120

D   135

4. A tailor has 315 yd of material.
He uses 3 yd to make a tablecloth.
Each tablecloth is sold for $4.
How much can he sell all the tablecloth for?

A $60

B $105

C $420

D $3780

5. There were 3056 men at a baseball match.
There were half as many women as men at the match.
There were 1000 fewer children than women.
How many children were at the match?

A   528

B   1528

C   2056

D   4056

Blank

20

Test A **Unit 4:** Multiplication Tables of 6, 7, 8 and 9

Chapter 1: Multiplying and Dividing by 6

What is 6 × 7? _____

Divide 54 by 6. _____

Write the missing number in each box.

[____] × 6 = 48

48 ÷ 6 = [____]

Look at the circles and write two multiplication sentences.

[____] × [____] = [____]

[____] × [____] = [____]

5. 54 flowers are put equally into 6 vases.
   How many flowers are there in each vase?

   There are _____ flowers in each vase.

6. Write the missing number in each box.

   (a) 6 × 10 is [   ] more than 6 × 9.

   (b) 6 × 9 = 60 − [   ] = [   ]

7. Multiply 327 by 6.
   Show your working below.

   The answer is _____.

8. What is the remainder when you divide 629 by 6?
   Show your working below.

   The remainder is _____.

Primary Mathematics (Standards Edition) Tests 3A

How would you check if the following is correct?

216 ÷ 6 = 36

Show your working below.

Is the answer correct? _____

. What is 252 × 6?
Show your working below.
Use estimation to check if your answer is reasonable.

Estimation

Is your answer reasonable? _____

. Yvonne has $2216.
She gives $75 each to 6 of her favorite charities.
She saves the rest.
How much does she save?

She saves $_____.

12. There are 930 blue and red flags altogether.
    There are 5 times as many blue flags as red flags.
    How many red flags are there?

    There are _____ red flags.

13. 6 television sets cost $7704.
    What is the cost of 5 such television sets?

    5 such television sets cost $_____.

Test B   **Unit 4:** Multiplication Tables of 6, 7, 8 and 9

Chapter 1: Multiplying and Dividing by 6

Circle the correct option, **A**, **B**, **C** or **D**.

6 × 6 is _____ more than 6 × 5.

A   1   **C**   30

B   6   **D**   36

Which division sentence is modeled by the figure?

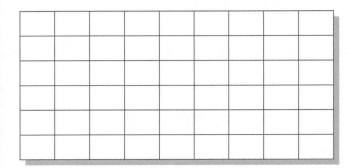

A   9 ÷ 3 = 3   **C**   45 ÷ 5 = 9

B   15 ÷ 3 = 5   **D**   54 ÷ 6 = 9

Lara bought 5 bouquets of roses.
If each bouquet cost $6, how much did she pay?

A $15   **C** $30

B $18   **D** $90

Turn the page.

08 Marshall Cavendish International (Singapore) Private Limited   Primary Mathematics (Standards Edition) Tests 3A

4. There are 27 students in a class.
   There are 6 classes.
   How many students are there?

   A   4 R 3   **C**   33

   B   21   **D**   162

5. Mrs. Kali works 6 hours a day.
   She earns $156 a day.
   How much does she earn in an hour?

   A $26   **C** $162

   B $150   **D** $936

6. Which of the following is the closest estimate for 9132 ×

   A   9000 × 6   **C**   10,000 × 6

   B   9500 ÷ 6   **D**   10,000 × 10

7. How would you check if the following is correct?

   1188 ÷ 6 = 198

   A   396 × 2 = 198   **C**   1100 + 88 = 1188

   B   198 × 6 = 1188   **D**   1980 − 792 = 1188

8. 750 men and 336 women were at a meeting.
   They got into groups of 6 for a discussion.
   How many groups were there?

   A   56   **C**   181

   B   125   **D**   1086

Mary and Jane made 90 red paper roses and 48 yellow ones.
They sold each paper rose for $6.
If they sold all the roses, how much did they collect in all?

A $15   C $138

B $23   D $828

. A calculator cost $21.
It cost 3 times as much as a stapler.
Mr. Stewart bought 6 staplers for his students.
How much did he pay?

A $7   C $63

B $42   D $126

. Look at the division problem.

6423 ÷ 6 = 1070 R 3

Which would you use to check if the answer is correct?

A   1070 × 6 = 6420 then 6420 + 3 = 6423

B   1070 × 5 = 5350 then 5350 + 1073 = 6423

C   6423 ÷ 3 = 2141 then 2141 + 4282 = 6423

D   713 × 9 = 6417 then 6417 + 6 = 6423

. Divide 1625 by 6.

A   27 R 5   C   270 R 5

B   270   D   9750

13. 6 library shelves hold 1500 books.
    How many books are there on 4 shelves?

    A   250   **C**   1000

    B   900   **D**   6000

14. 822 adults and 6 times as many children attended a
    concert over 3 days.
    If the same number of people attended the concert each
    day, how many children attended each day?

    A   1644   **C**   2466

    B   1918   **D**   4932

15. There are 108 fish tanks in a shop.
    The shopkeeper puts 6 guppies into each tank.

    There are **about** _____ guppies altogether.

    A   400   **C**   600

    B   500   **D**   1000

Primary Mathematics (Standards Edition) Tests 3A   © 2008 Marshall Cavendish International (Singapore) Private Lir

Test A

Unit 4: Multiplication Tables of 6, 7, 8 and 9

Chapter 2: Multiplying and Dividing by 7

Write the missing number in each box.

Number of boxes	1	2	3	4	5	6		8	9	
Number of pencils	7	14		28	35	42	49	56		70

Write two multiplication sentences for the triangles.

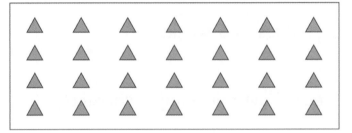

☐ × ☐ = ☐

☐ × ☐ = ☐

Write the missing number in each box.

☐ × 7 = 21

21 ÷ 7 = ☐

4. Write the missing number in each box.

    (a) $7 \times 10 =$ ☐

    (b) $7 \times 9 =$ ☐ $- 7 =$ ☐

5. $9 \times$ _____ $= 63$

6. How many days are there in 6 weeks?

    There are _____ days in 6 weeks.

7. How would you check if the following is correct?

    $98 \div 7 = 14$

    Show your working below.

    Is the answer correct? _____

8. Craig sold 362 fruits every day.
    How many fruits did he sell in a week?

    He sold _____ fruits in a week.

Primary Mathematics (Standards Edition) Tests 3A

8178 roses were packed in boxes of 7.
How many boxes were needed?
How many roses were left?

_____ boxes were needed.

_____ roses were left.

). There are 14 flowers in 7 boxes.
Each flower costs $6.
How much does a box of flowers cost?

A box of flowers costs $_____.

11. 7 bags cost $735.
    How much do 4 such bags cost?

    4 such bags cost $_____.

12. There are 378 students in a school.
    There are 6 times as many boys as girls.
    How many girls are there?

    There are _____ girls.

Primary Mathematics (Standards Edition) Tests 3A

10

Test B   Unit 4: Multiplication Tables of 6, 7, 8 and 9

Chapter 2: Multiplying and Dividing by 7

Circle the correct option, **A**, **B**, **C** or **D**.

What is 7 × 7?

A   0   **C**   14

B   1   **D**   49

What are the missing numbers in the table below?

Number of tanks	1	2	3	4	5	Q
Amount of water (liters)	7	14	P	28	35	42

A   P: 15, Q: 6   **C**   P: 21, Q: 6

B   P: 15, Q: 7   **D**   P: 21, Q: 7

Which of the following is the closest estimate for 42 × 7?

A   40 × 7 = 280   **C**   40 × 10 = 400

B   50 × 7 = 350   **D**   50 × 10 = 500

May spent $84 on 7 kg of chicken.
How much did 1 kg of chicken cost?

A $10   **C** $91

B $12   **D** $588

5. Mr. Lee worked 276 days.
    How many weeks and days did he work?

    A   30 weeks 6 days   **C**   39 weeks 4 days

    B   39 weeks 3 days   **D**   40 weeks

6. A tailor had 216 m of cloth.
    He used 7 m of cloth to make a suit.
    He made as many similar suits as possible.
    How much cloth did he have left?

    A   1 m   **C**   6 m

    B   5 m   **D**   30 m

7. If 7 bags cost $392, how much would 5 such bags cost?

    A $56   **C** $404

    B $280   **D** $548

8. Jumu has 644 red beads.
    She has 7 times as many red beads as black beads.
    She has 4 times as many black beads as white beads.
    How many white beads does she have?

    A   23   **C**   368

    B   92   **D**   4508

9. Every month, Judy donated $470 to a children's charity and
    $384 to the Heart Association.
    She donated to both charities for 7 months.
    How much did she donate altogether?

    A $854   **C** $3290

    B $2680   **D** $5978

Primary Mathematics (Standards Edition) Tests 3A

). Alan was paid $7 an hour for gardening.
He was paid $224 for four days of gardening work.
He worked 8 hours on Monday, 9 hours on Tuesday and
7 hours on Wednesday.
How many hours did he work on Thursday?

A 4 hours   **C** 24 hours

B 8 hours   **D** 32 hours

Blank

Unit 4: Multiplication Tables of 6, 7, 8 and 9

Chapter 3: Multiplying and Dividing by 8

Fill in the blanks.

No. of days	1	2	**A**	4	5	6	7
No. of hours worked	8	16	24	32	40	48	**B**

A is _____.

B is _____.

Look at the circles.
Write a multiplication sentence and a division sentence using the multiplication table of 8.

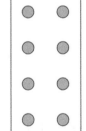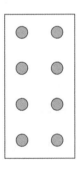

$\boxed{} \times \boxed{} = \boxed{}$

$\boxed{} \div \boxed{} = \boxed{}$

Write 8 × 6 as a repeated addition sentence.

_____

©08 Marshall Cavendish International (Singapore) Private Limited   Primary Mathematics (Standards Edition) Tests 3A

4. Habi drew 3 portraits in a day.
   He drew the same number of portraits each day for 8 day
   How many portraits did he draw in all?

   He drew _____ portraits.

5. Janice uses 28 beads to make a necklace.
   How many beads does she use to make 8 necklaces?

   28 × 8 = ☐

   She uses _____ beads.

   Use estimation to check if your answer is reasonable.

Estimation

   Is your answer reasonable? _____

Look at the following division problem.

272 ÷ 8 = 34

How would you check if the answer is correct?
Show your working below.

Is the answer correct? _____

Brandon saves $720 of his salary every month.
How much will he save in 8 months?

He will save $_____ in 8 months.

827 ÷ 8 = _____

Fill in the ◯ with **<**, **>** or **=**.

729 ÷ 9 ◯ 9 × 9

10. How would you check the following division problem?

```
        8 0 2
    8)6 4 1 9
      6 4
        0 1
        0 0
          1 9
          1 6
          0 3
```

Show your working below.

11. A basketball cost $8.
    A coach bought 21 basketballs.
    He paid $200.
    How much change did he receive?

He received $_____ in change.

Primary Mathematics (Standards Edition) Tests 3A   © 2008 Marshall Cavendish International (Singapore) Private Lin

2. A tank held 528 liters of petrol.
   The petrol was poured into 8 smaller containers to be delivered to petrol kiosks.
   One of the petrol kiosks needed only 36 liters of petrol.
   How much petrol was left in the container that went to that kiosk?

   _____ liters of petrol was left.

3. Stephanie ordered 3456 buns for a school party.
   8 buns cost $7.
   How much did she pay?

   She paid $_____.

©2008 Marshall Cavendish International (Singapore) Private Limited

14. A television set cost $3147.
    Mr. Chan paid $360 every month for 8 months.
    How much more would he have to pay after 8 months?

He would have to pay $_____ more.

Primary Mathematics (Standards Edition) Tests 3A

Test B **Unit 4:** Multiplication Tables of 6, 7, 8 and 9

Chapter 3: Multiplying and Dividing by 8

Circle the correct option, **A**, **B**, **C** or **D**.

What is a division sentence for $8 \times 2 = 16$?

A $16 \div 10 = 1 \text{ R } 6$ **C** $16 \div 4 = 4$

B $16 \div 8 = 2$ **D** $8 \div 2 = 4$

What is the missing number?

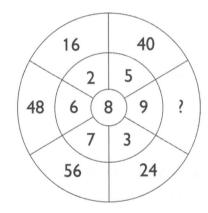

A   8   **C**   72

B   32   **D**   80

$616 \div 8 = $ _____

A   77   **C**   624

B   608   **D**   4928

4. Katherine bought 8 books for $336.
   How much did 1 book cost?

       A $42   **C** $344

       B $328   **D** $2688

5. 8549 ÷ 8 = _____

       A   168 R 3   **C**   1068 R 3

       B   168 R 5   **D**   1068 R 5

6. Which sign belongs in the ◯ ?

   32 × 8 ◯ 2024 ÷ 8

       A   >   **C**   <

       B   =   **D**   –

7. There were 8 erasers in a box.
   Each eraser was sold at $1.
   A salesperson sold 59 such boxes of erasers.
   How much did he get altogether?

       A $8   **C** $472

       B $59   **D** $480

8. 4760 people were at a party.
   There were 7 times as many men as women.
   How many women were there?

       A   595   **C**   1275

       B   680   **D**   4767

Primary Mathematics (Standards Edition) Tests 3A   © 2008 Marshall Cavendish International (Singapore) Private Lim.

A gold ring cost $1792.
The gold ring cost 7 times as much as a silver ring.
How much did the two rings cost in all?

A $224   **C** $2048

B $256   **D** $3584

. A circus collected $4384 on its opening day and twice as
much the next day.
If each ticket cost $8, how many people attended the
circus on the second day?

A   548   **C**   1644

B   1096   **D**   8768

8 Marshall Cavendish International (Singapore) Private Limited

Blank

Test A

Unit 4: Multiplication Tables of 6, 7, 8 and 9

Chapter 4: Multiplying and Dividing by 9

Fill in the blanks.

9 × 9 = 90 – _____ = _____

Write the missing number in each box.

72 ÷ 9 = [ ]

9 × [ ] = 72

Write the missing number in the box.

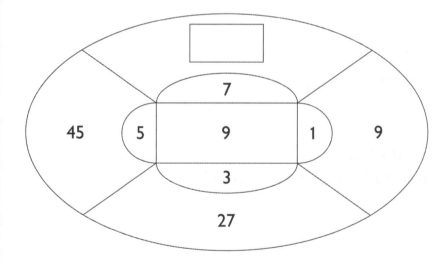

4. What is shown by the circles below?
   Write a multiplication sentence.

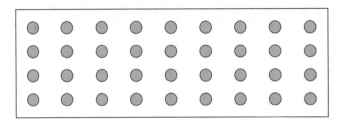

   [ ] × [ ] = [ ]

5. Divide 725 by 9.
   Show your working below.

   The answer is _____.

6. A radio costs $127.
   How much do 9 such radios cost?

   9 radios cost $_____.

Divide.

$$9\overline{)9179}$$

Quotient = _____   Remainder = _____

Estimate the value of 478 × 9.

┌─────────────────────────┐
│   Estimation   │
│   │
│   │
│   │
│   │
│   │
│   │
└─────────────────────────┘

478 × 9 is about _____.

There are 9 classes of students.
There are 10 boys and 8 more girls than boys
in each class.
How many students are there altogether?

There are _____ students altogether.

8 Marshall Cavendish International (Singapore) Private Limited

Primary Mathematics (Standards Edition) Tests 3A

10. Valerie baked 216 butter cookies and
189 almond cookies.
She sold each cookie at 9¢ each.
How much did she get if she sold all the cookies?

She got _____¢.

11. A table costs 9 times as much as a chair.
A chair costs 3 times as much as a cushion.
If the table costs $1215, how much does the
cushion cost?

The cushion costs $_____.

2. There are 509 people waiting to board a van.
   The van can only take 9 people at a time.
   How many trips must the van make so that all the people
   can be transported?

The van must make _____ trips.

3. There are 9 apples and 9 oranges in a crate.
   An apple costs $3 and an orange costs $2.
   How much does a crate of apples and oranges cost?

It costs $_____.

08 Marshall Cavendish International (Singapore) Private Limited

Blank

Test B

Unit 4: Multiplication Tables of 6, 7, 8 and 9

Chapter 4: Multiplying and Dividing by 9

Circle the correct option, **A, B, C** or **D**.

Which number belongs in the box?

$63 \div \boxed{} = 7$

A	7	**C**	70
B	9	**D**	441

Divide 98 by 9.

A	1 R 8	**C**	10 R 8
B	1 R 9	**D**	10 R 9

Multiply 615 by 9.

A	69	**C**	624
B	606	**D**	5535

Which of the following is the closest estimate for 1326 × 9?

A	1000 × 9	**C**	2000 × 9
B	1500 ÷ 9	**D**	2000 × 10

Which of the following numbers can be divided exactly by both 8 and 9?

A	152	**C**	306
B	216	**D**	453

6. Divide 5327 by 9.

   A   532 R 7   **C**   591 R 8

   B   591 R 1   **D**   600

7. The length of a rod is 522 cm.
   It is painted black and white as shown below.

   What is the length of one black segment and one white segment?

   A   58 cm   **B**   116 cm   **C**   232 cm   **D**   290 cm

8. Jadi made 9 chains.
   Each chain had 156 beads.
   After making the chains, she still had 362 beads left.
   How many beads did she have at first?

   A   518   **B**   1042   **C**   1404   **D**   1766

9. Mr. Lee is 9 years older than his wife.
   His wife is 9 times as old as their son.
   If Mr. Lee is 54 years old, how old is his son?

   A   5   **B**   6   **C**   45   **D**   72

10. A painting cost $3654.
    At an art exhibition, 2 such paintings were sold.
    The total cost was paid over a period of 9 months.
    What was the amount paid each month?

    A $406   **B** $812   **C** $1827   **D** $7308

Test A

Unit 4: Multiplication Tables of 6, 7, 8 and 9

Chapter 5: More Multiplication and Division

Write a multiplication sentence about the circles below.

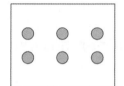 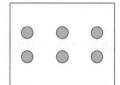 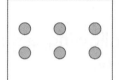 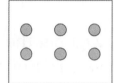

$$\boxed{} \times \boxed{} \times \boxed{} = \boxed{}$$

Fill in the blanks.

(a) $7 \times 2 \times 6 =$ _____ $\times\, 6 =$ _____

(b) $50 \times 7 \times 2 =$ _____ $\times\, 7 =$ _____

If $19 \times 2 \times 6 = 228$, what is $6 \times 19 \times 2?$ _____

What is $25 \times 9 \times 8?$ _____

Use mental calculation to find the value of the following.

(a) $9000 \div 3 =$ _____

(b) 16 hundreds divided by 4 _____

6. Estimate the value of 362 ÷ 7.

   _____ ÷ 7 = _____

   362 ÷ 7 is about _____.

7. Zigi did the following estimation to check if her answer was reasonable.

   4500 ÷ 9 = 500

   Circle the problem she could have been doing.

   3619 ÷ 9   4012 ÷ 9   5345 ÷ 9

8. Mary has 22 red beads and 8 times as many blue beads. How many beads does she have in all?

   She has _____ beads in all.

Primary Mathematics (Standards Edition) Tests 3A   © 2008 Marshall Cavendish International (Singapore) Private Lin

6 chairs were selling for $1938 at a store.

(a) Estimate the cost of each chair.

Each chair cost about $_____.

(b) Mrs. Remo brought $900 to the store.
About how many chairs could she buy?

She could buy about _____ chairs.

10. There are 280 boys in a school.
    There are twice as many girls as boys in the school.

    (a) How many girls are there?

    There are _____ girls.

    (b) The girls are put into groups of 9.
        Estimate the number of groups formed.

    About _____ groups of girls are formed.

15

Test B

Unit 4: Multiplication Tables of 6, 7, 8 and 9

Chapter 5: More Multiplication and Division

Circle the correct option, **A**, **B**, **C** or **D**.

1. Which of the following shows 6 × 3 × 4?

A

B

C

D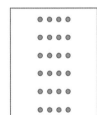

2. What is 9 times of 54?

A   6   **C**   63

B   45   **D**   486

179

3. Which number belongs in the box?

$$240 \div \boxed{} = 30$$

A   3   C   6

B   4   D   8

4. If $5 \times 9 \times 15 = 675$, what is $15 \times 5 \times 9$?

A   45   C   135

B   75   D   675

5. Which number belongs in the box?

$$12 \times 7 \times 8 = \boxed{}$$

A   56   C   96

B   84   D   672

6. Which sign belongs in the $\bigcirc$?

$$2 \times 4 \times 8 \;\bigcirc\; 3 \times 3 \times 7$$

A   >   C   <

B   =   D   +

7. Which number belongs in each box?

$$20 \times \boxed{} \times \boxed{} = 640$$

A   2; 6   C   4; 8

B   3; 4   D   0; 32

Primary Mathematics (Standards Edition) Tests 3A

$3200 \div 8 =$ _____

A 4

C 400

B 40

D 4000

Which number belongs in each box?

$48 \div \boxed{P} = 8$

$480 \div 6 = \boxed{Q}$

$\boxed{R} \div 6 = 800$

A P: 6, Q: 80, R: 4800

C P: 6, Q: 48, R: 8000

B P: 8, Q: 60, R: 4800

D P: 8, Q: 80, R: 8000

0. What is 20 hundreds divided by 5?

A 1 hundred

C 40 hundreds

B 4 hundreds

D 100 hundreds

. Use mental calculation to find the value of $6400 \div 8$.

A 8

C 720

B 80

D 800

2. Shane read 9 books in January.
He read 3 times as many books in February as in January.
He read twice as many books in March as in February.
How many books did he read in March?

A 18

C 36

B 27

D 54

13. There are 322 boys in a school.
    The boys are divided equally into 8 groups.
    Estimate the number of boys in each group.

    A   30   **C**   50

    B   40   **D**   80

14. Estimate the value of 617 ÷ 6.

    A   100   **C**   300

    B   200   **D**   600

15. A shopkeeper collected $5932 over 3 days.
    Estimate how much he collected each day.

    A $500   **C** $2000

    B $1000   **D** $6000

Primary Mathematics (Standards Edition) Tests 3A
© 2008 Marshall Cavendish International (Singapore) Private Lim

Units 1–4

Arrange the numbers in order.
Begin with the smallest.

2815, 6002, 2185, 5993

_____

If today is Wednesday, 21st July, what is the date the
following Friday?

_____

There are 562 oranges.
There are 79 more oranges than kiwi fruit.
How many kiwi fruit are there?

There are _____ kiwi fruit.

4. 1942 people went to the Science Center on Monday.
   2465 people went on Tuesday.
   Round the number of visitors to the nearest thousand.
   Then estimate the total number of people who went to th
   Science Center on the two days.

   About _____ people went to the Science Center.

5. Look at the following numbers below.
   Write the next number sentence in the sequence.

   15 − 8 = 7
   25 − 8 = 17
   35 − 8 = 27
   45 − 8 = 37

   ☐ − ☐ = ☐

6. Shade to show 8 × 4 in the grid below.

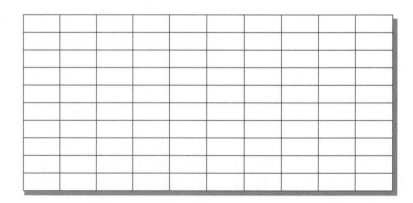

Primary Mathematics (Standards Edition) Tests 3A   © 2008 Marshall Cavendish International (Singapore) Private Lir

The following shows 3 × 6.

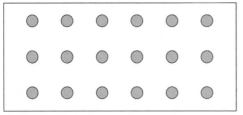

Show 8 × 7 in the box below.

8 × 7 = _____

There are **29** girls in one class.
There are **6** classes.
How many girls are there in all?

There are _____ girls in all.

Primary Mathematics (Standards Edition) Tests 3A

9. Fill in the box with **T** if the statement is true, or **F** if the statement is false.

(a) $217 \times 0 = 217$ ☐

(b) $0 \div 0 = 1$ ☐

(c) $76 \div 1 = 76$ ☐

(d) $19 \times 1 = 19$ ☐

10. Find the product of 365 and 6.

The answer is _____.

11. Fill in the ◯ with **>**, **<** or **=**.

12×6 ◯ 8×9 ◯ $70 + 2$

12. Divide 817 by 8.

The quotient is _____.

The remainder is _____.

Primary Mathematics (Standards Edition) Tests 3A

. How would you check if the following answer is correct?

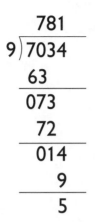

Show your working below.

. Peter has 5 times as much money as Steve.
They have $216 altogether.
How much does Steve have?

Steve has $_____.

15. Julie has $434.
    She has 7 times as much as Patrick.
    How much do they have altogether?

    They have $_____ altogether.

16. There are 365 days in a year.
    Estimate the number of weeks there are in a year.

    There are about _____ weeks in a year.

17. Mary has $56.
    She has an equal number of $2 and $5 notes.
    How many $5 notes does she have?
    Use the table and the example to help you.

$2 notes	$5 notes	Total amount
6	6	$12 + $30 = $42

    She has _____ $5 notes.

Primary Mathematics (Standards Edition) Tests 3A

3. Find the value of $\triangle$.

$\triangle \times 6 = \bigcirc$

$\bigcirc + 15 = \square$

$\square \div 7 = \stackrel{\star}{}$

$\stackrel{\star}{} - 9 = 12$

The value of $\triangle$ is _____.

4. Kwami bought a refrigerator for $3419.
He paid $1939 in the first month and the remaining
amount over a period of 8 months.
He paid an equal amount each month.
How much did he pay each month?

He paid $_____ each month.

20. A notebook cost $2, a magnifying glass cost $5 and an eraser set cost $3.
John bought 4 notebooks, 5 magnifying glasses and 3 sets of erasers.
How much did he pay?

He paid $_____.

20

Cumulative Test B   **Units 1–4**

ircle the correct option, **A**, **B**, **C** or **D**.

Travis estimated the number of cards in his shop at 7600.
How many cards could there actually be?

A   6974   **C**   7660

B   7582   **D**   7721

Which of the following describes the numbers in the boxes
correctly?

| 1749 | 1479 | 7419 |

A   1749 > 1479 < 7419   **C**   1479 < 7419 < 1749

B   7419 > 1749 < 1479   **D**   1479 < 1749 < 7419

Which sign belongs in the $\bigcirc$?

$6 \times 6 \bigcirc 5 \times 7$

A   >   **C**   <

B   =   **D**   +

There are 566 men at a conference.
There are 187 more men than women.
How many women are there?

A   379   **C**   643

B   421   **D**   753

8 Marshall Cavendish International (Singapore) Private Limited   Primary Mathematics (Standards Edition) Tests 3A

5. Subtract 2214 from 7000.

   A 4786   **C** 5214

   B 4896   **D** 9214

6. Multiply 400 by 9.

   A 36   **C** 1300

   B 360   **D** 3600

7. $372 \times 4 =$ _____

   A 93   **C** 376

   B 368   **D** 1488

8. Which number belongs in the box?

   ☐ $\div\ 3 = 63\ R\ 2$

   A 21   **C** 189

   B 23   **D** 191

9. A bag costs 7 times as much as a pair of shoes.
   If the bag costs $392, how much is the pair of shoes?

   A $56   **C** $399

   B $385   **D** $2744

10. Joseph made 1765 tarts in 5 days.
    He made the same number of tarts every day.
    How many tarts did he make on the last day?

    A 353   **C** 1770

    B 1760   **D** 8825

Primary Mathematics (Standards Edition) Tests 3A

© 2008 Marshall Cavendish International (Singapore) Private Li

1. How would you check if the following is correct?

   1473 ÷ 8 = 184 R 1

   A   184 × 1 then subtract 8   **C**   184 × 8 then subtract 1
   B   184 × 1 then add 8   **D**   184 × 8 then add 1

2. Which is the missing number in the box?

   28 × ☐ × 2 = 336

   A   6   **C**   12
   B   7   **D**   168

3. Estimate the value of 4621 ÷ 7.

   A   500   **C**   700
   B   600   **D**   800

4. 5 apples cost $6.
   How much do 35 apples cost?

   A $5   **C** $42
   B $30   **D** $46

5. 10 shirts cost $830.
   How much do 7 such shirts cost?

   A $83   **C** $813
   B $581   **D** $837

6. A china doll cost $657.
   It cost 9 times as much as a lampshade.
   How much did Mrs. Allen pay for both items?

   A $73   **B** $730   **C** $5913   **D** $6570

17. A factory produced 1792 blue mugs and 600 more yellow mugs than blue ones.
    The yellow mugs were packed into boxes of 8.
    How many boxes were needed?

    A 75   **C** 299

    B 224   **D** 2392

18. Cindy has 6 times as many cards as Dennis.
    Dennis has half as many cards as Lucy.
    They have 648 cards altogether.
    How many cards does Dennis have?

    A 54   **C** 108

    B 72   **D** 324

19. Jim has 7 more red pens than blue pens in his shop.
    He has 259 pens altogether.
    How many blue pens does he have?

    A 126   **C** 249

    B 133   **D** 266

20. Wallace had 742 cards.
    After he gave 32 of them to Freya, they had the same number of cards.
    How many cards did Freya have at first?

    A 387   **C** 710

    B 678   **D** 774

Test A

Unit 5: Data Analysis

Chapter 1: Presenting Data

Use the tally chart to answer the questions that follow.

Groups of people who visited the Discovery Center	Number of people
Men	卌 卌 ||
Women	卌 卌 卌
Boys	卌 卌 卌 |||
Girls	卌 卌	

(a) Which group of people was there most of?

_____

(b) How many adults were there?

_____

(c) How many females were there?

_____

(d) How many more boys than men were there?

_____

195

2. Use the bar graph to answer the questions that follow. The data shows the number of fruits at a store.

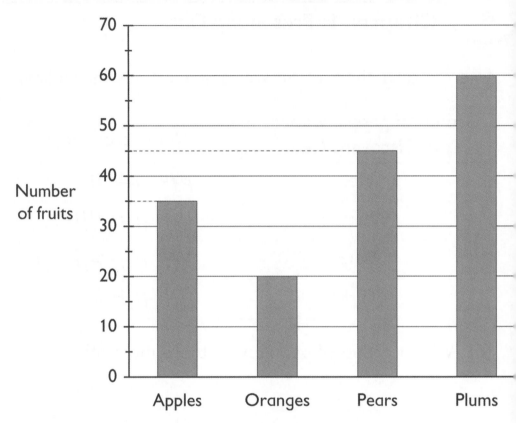

(a) Which fruit is there most of?

_____

(b) How many more plums than apples are there?

_____

(c) How many fruits are there altogether?

_____

Primary Mathematics (Standards Edition) Tests 3A

Use the table to answer the questions that follow.

Name	Red beads	White beads
Amy	12	10
Benson	21	5
Charles	16	14
Dillon	9	20

(a) Who has the most number of beads?

_____

(b) How many more red than white beads does
Benson have?

_____

(c) Benson has more beads than _____.

He has _____ more beads.

(d) Which two people have a total of 25 red beads?

_____

4. Complete the table and answer the questions that follow.

	Section A	Section B	Total number of questions
Test A	7		21
Test B		15	
Total number of questions		29	48

(a) How many fewer questions are there in Test A than in Test B?

_____

(b) Which section of the tests has more questions?

_____

(c) Each question in Test B is worth 2 points. What is the total score for Test B?

_____

Primary Mathematics (Standards Edition) Tests 3A   © 2008 Marshall Cavendish International (Singapore) Private Limi

The data shows the amount of money each student saved.
Look at the example of Janet's data and complete the
line plot.

	Number of dollars saved
Linsy	⏤⏤ ⏤⏤ ||
Francis	⏤⏤
Gerry	⏤⏤ ||||
Harry	⏤⏤ ⏤⏤ ⏤⏤
Janet	|||

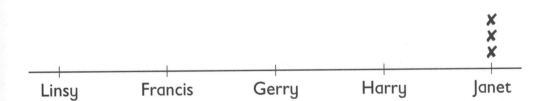

(a) Who saved the most? _____

   How much did he/she save? _____

(b) How much more did Linsy save than Gerry? _____

2008 Marshall Cavendish International (Singapore) Private Limited

6. A survey was done on the T-shirt colors that students liked.

   Each student chose only one color.

   Look at the data and complete the table.

(R) : red	(G) : green
(B) : blue	(Y) : yellow

(R) (B) (B) (R) (R) (Y) (G)

(B) (B) (Y) (G) (R) (R)

(R) (G) (B) (G) (R) (R)

(Y) (R) (G) (B) (Y) (G)

Colors	Tally	Number of students
Red		
Blue		
Green		
Yellow		

(a) How many students were surveyed? _____

(b) Which color was the most popular? _____

(c) Which color was the least popular? _____

Primary Mathematics (Standards Edition) Tests 3A

Test B

Unit 5: Data Analysis

Chapter 1: Presenting Data

Circle the correct option, **A**, **B**, **C** or **D**.

Use the graph below to answer questions 1 and 2.
The data shows the Science scores of four students.

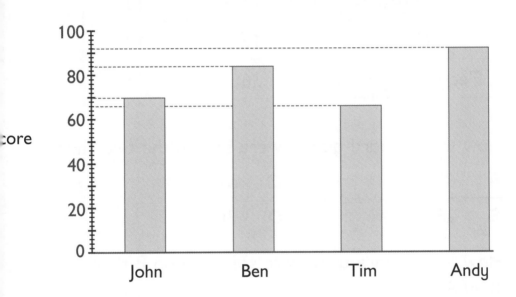

Score

John   Ben   Tim   Andy

1. What is the difference between the highest and lowest scores?

   A   18   **C**   66

   B   26   **D**   92

2. How many more points than John and Ben put together did Tim and Andy put together score?

   A   1   **C**   11

   B   4   **D**   15

© 2008 Marshall Cavendish International (Singapore) Private Limited

Use the table below to answer questions 3 and 4.
The table shows the number of toys and games sold at shops A and B.

Toys and Games	Shop A	Shop B
Dolls	10	18
Board games	21	15
Cars	12	17
Electronic games	36	31

3. How many board games were sold in the two shops?

    A 6   **C** 31

    B 28   **D** 36

4. How many more toys were sold in shop B than in shop A?

    A 2   **C** 79

    B 8   **D** 81

Use the table below to answer questions 5 to 7.
The tally chart shows the number of different towels sold.

Towels	Number sold
Hand towels	ＩＩＩＩ ＩＩＩＩ ＩＩＩＩ
Bath towels	ＩＩＩＩ Ｉ
Floor towels	ＩＩＩＩ ＩＩＩＩ ＩＩＩＩ ＩＩ

Primary Mathematics (Standards Edition) Tests 3A   © 2008 Marshall Cavendish International (Singapore) Private Lim

How many more floor towels than hand towels were sold?

A 3 **B** 6 **C** 8 **D** 11

How many towels were sold altogether?

A 20 **B** 23 **C** 31 **D** 37

Which graph represents the data in the tally chart?

A

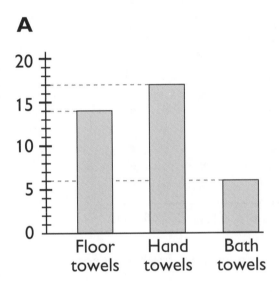

C

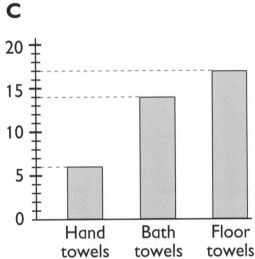

B

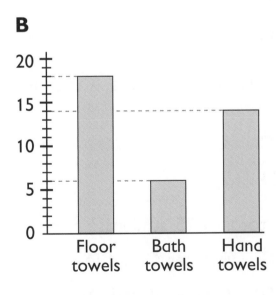

D

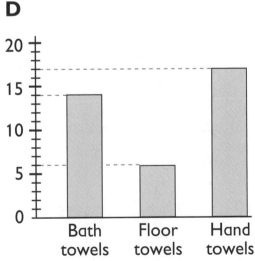

Use the line plot below to answer questions 8 to 10.
The graph shows the number of students in four classes.

8. How many students are there in the four classes?

    A   18   **C**   43

    B   32   **D**   58

9. How many more students are there in Class A than in
    Class D?

    A   1   **C**   4

    B   3   **D**   7

10. Which two classes have a total of 25 students?

    A   Classes A and B   **C**   Classes C and D

    B   Classes B and C   **D**   Classes B and D

Primary Mathematics (Standards Edition) Tests 3A   © 2008 Marshall Cavendish International (Singapore) Private Limit

Points

15

Test A

Unit 5: Data Analysis

Chapter 2: Probability

Sally has a box of 10 red balls and 5 yellow balls.
She picks one ball at a time without looking into the box.
State whether the events below are **certain**, **likely**,
unlikely or **impossible**.

(a) Sally picks a blue ball from the box. _____

(b) Sally picks a red ball from the box. _____

(c) Sally picks a colored ball. _____

(d) Sally picks a yellow ball. _____

The stars below represent the number of black stars and
white stars that some children pick out of a bag.

(a) Record the above data in the tally chart.

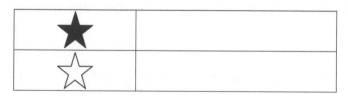

(b) If a child picks out another star, it is likely to be a

_____ star.

3. Zechariah picks the following black, gray and white balls from a box.

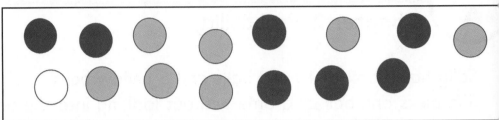

(a) He is unlikely to pick a _____ ball.

(b) He is just as likely to pick a _____ ball as a _____ ball.

4. The table shows the data of three Grade 1 students. Fill in the blanks with **certain**, **likely**, **unlikely** or **impossible**.

Name	Height	Weight
Sandy	135 cm	36 kg
Jonathan	142 cm	39 kg
Penny	139 cm	38 kg

(a) Tom, who is from the same grade, is 170 cm tall.

_____

(b) Lucy, who is from the same grade, weighs 3 kg.

_____

(c) Dexter, who is from the same grade, is 140 cm tal

_____

Janice spins a spinner and the results are recorded.

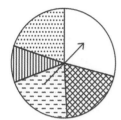

‖‖ ‖	‖‖ ‖‖	‖‖	‖‖ ‖	‖‖

(a) Draw a bar graph to represent the data in the tally chart.

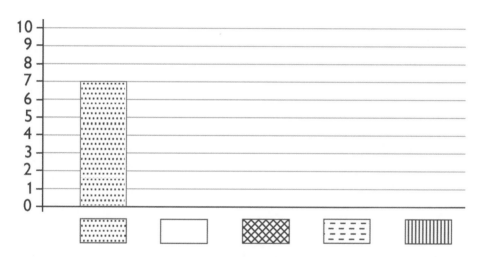

Check ✔ the correct box for each question.

(b) Which section is the spinner most likely to land on?

(c) Which section is the spinner **next** most likely to land on?

Blank

Test B

Unit 5: Data Analysis

Chapter 2: Probability

Circle the correct option, **A**, **B**, **C** or **D**.

"The 4th of July falls on a Monday."

It is _____ that this will happen.

A   certain   **C**   unlikely

B   likely   **D**   impossible

A lucky dip has cards with prizes written on it.

Prize cards	Number of cards
"Thank you"	100
"A canned drink"	50
"A box of tissue"	50
"$100"	1

You are unlikely to get the _____ card.

A   "Thank you"   **C**   "$100"

B   "A box of tissue"   **D**   "A canned drink"

Turn the page.

Four color choices were given to some boys.
Each boy chose only one color.
The results were shown below.
Use the tally chart to answer questions 3 and 4.

Blue	ⵑⵑⵑⵑⵑ ⵑⵑⵑⵑⵑ //
Red	/
Yellow	ⵑⵑⵑⵑⵑ
Green	ⵑⵑⵑⵑⵑ ///

3. How many boys preferred blue to yellow?

A   5   **C**   12

B   7   **D**   17

4. According to the results, a boy was _____ to choose red

A   certain   **C**   unlikely

B   likely   **D**   impossible

coin is tossed twice each time and the results are shown below.

se the results to answer questions 5 to 7.

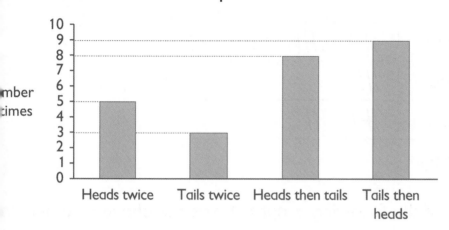

Which tally charts shows the results?

A

Heads twice	✝✝ ‖
Tails twice	✝✝
Heads then tails	✝✝ ‖‖
Tails then heads	‖‖

C

Heads twice	✝✝
Tails twice	‖‖
Heads then tails	✝✝ ‖‖
Tails then heads	✝✝ ‖‖‖

B

Heads twice	✝✝ ‖‖‖
Tails twice	‖‖
Heads then tails	✝✝ ‖‖
Tails then heads	‖‖

D

Heads twice	‖‖
Tails twice	✝✝
Heads then tails	✝✝ ‖
Tails then heads	✝✝ ‖‖‖

The coin landed most as _____.

A	Heads twice	**C**	Heads then tails
B	Tails twice	**D**	Tails then heads

If you are asked to guess what the toss will be, you are unlikely to guess _____.

A	Heads twice	**C**	Heads then tails
B	Tails twice	**D**	Tails then heads

The weather was recorded for the month of June.
Use the data in the tally chart below to answer questions 8 to 1

Sunny	ЖЖ ЖЖ ЖЖ ЖЖ
Rainy	|||
Cloudy	ЖЖ |||
Stormy	

8. Which of the following graphs shows the above weather da

A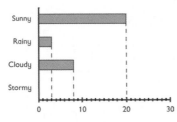

C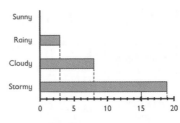

B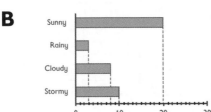

D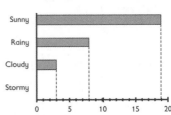

9. It is most likely to be _____ in June.

   A   sunny   **C**   rainy

   B   cloudy   **D**   stormy

10. How many more sunny days than cloudy days were there

   A   8   **C**   16

   B   12   **D**   19

Primary Mathematics (Standards Edition) Tests 3A

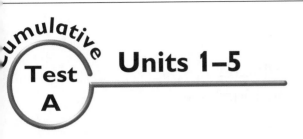

Cumulative Test A — Units 1–5

. Write the **greatest** 4-digit number you can make using all the digits below.
(Use each digit only once. Do not begin the number with 0.)

8, 0, 5, 6

_____

. What could the missing numbers be?

19 + ☐ < 40 < ☐ − 18

. Some classes brought in newspapers for recycling.
Class A brought 2 kg, Class B brought 3 kg more than
Class A and Class C brought as much as Classes A and B
put together.
How many kilograms of newspapers did they bring
altogether?

They brought _____ kg of newspapers altogether.

213

4. Victoria has $2178.
   She has $1542 more than Matthew.
   James has $6318 more than Matthew.
   How much does James have?

   James has $_____.

5. Write a division sentence that models the figure below.

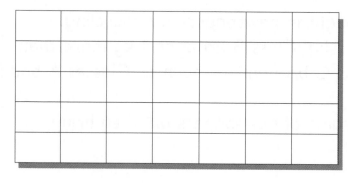

   _____

Primary Mathematics (Standards Edition) Tests 3A   © 2008 Marshall Cavendish International (Singapore) Private Limited

(a) There are 3 feet of material in 1 yard.
     How many feet of material are there in 12 yards?

     There are _____ feet of material.

(b) 1 foot is 12 inches long.
     How many inches is a 4-foot ruler?

     It is _____ inches long.

. A cab can carry a maximum of 4 people.
  217 people took cabs.
  Each cab carried the maximum number before the next
  one was hired.
  How many cabs were used to carry **all** the people?

  _____ cabs were used.

. If 56 × 7 × 9 = 3528, what is 9 × 56 × 7? _____

Use the graph below to answer questions 9 to 11.
The survey shows how students go to school.
Each student is allowed to choose only one mode of transport

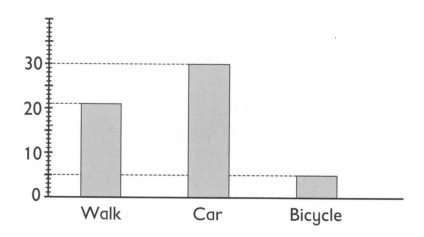

9.   How do most students go to school? _____

10. How many more students go to school by car than by

     walking? _____

11. How many students were surveyed? _____

Primary Mathematics (Standards Edition) Tests 3A   © 2008 Marshall Cavendish International (Singapore) Private Limite

se the table to answer questions 12 to 14.
he data shows how many pages were printed by some machines.

	Morning	Afternoon
Machine A	320	540
Machine B	137	215
Machine C	426	334

2. How many pages were printed by Machine B? _____

3. Which machine printed more, A or B? _____

   How many pages more? _____

4. How many pages did the machines print in the

   afternoon? _____

Turn the page. >

Refer to the graph to answer questions 15 to 17.
The data shows the number of students who read 0 to 6 book
in a week.

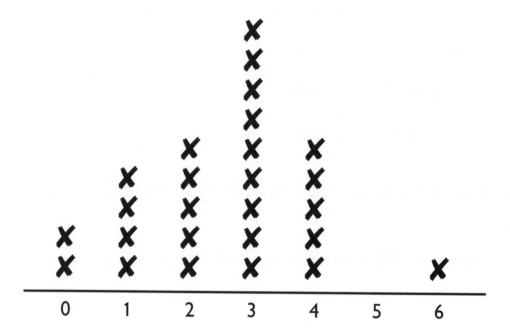

15. What is the number of books read by most of the students

_____

16. Elizabeth reads 4 books in a week.
    Put a ✗ in the graph to add Elizabeth's data.

17. Including Elizabeth, how many students read more than
    2 books in a week?

_____

Primary Mathematics (Standards Edition) Tests 3A   © 2008 Marshall Cavendish International (Singapore) Private Limite

8. There are some colored rings in a bag.

Yellow	3
Green	10
Blue	2

Cindy picks a ring from the bag without looking.
Which color is she most likely to pick? _____

9. Fill in the blanks with **certain, likely, unlikely** or **impossible**.

A regular six-sided die is rolled.

(a) Will the number be more than 4?

_____

(b) Will the number be less than 7?

_____

(c) Will the number be a 2-digit number?

_____

(d) Will the number be a single-digit number?

_____

Primary Mathematics (Standards Edition) Tests 3A

Blank

Cumulative Test B — Units 1–5

7020 in words is _____.

A seventy twenty

B seven hundred twenty

C seven thousand, two

D seven thousand, twenty

Which digit belongs in the box?

25☐3 < 2560

A 7   **C** 6

B 3   **D** 9

Which would you use to check if the answer is correct?

527 − 87 = 440

A 440 + 87   **C** 527 + 87

B 440 − 87   **D** 527 − 440

Alison wants to buy a coat for $76, a pair of shoes for $59, a luggage bag for $275 and a wallet for $8.
She has $400 and wants to spend as much of her money as possible.
Which item will she **not** buy?

A coat   **C** shoes

B bag   **D** wallet

08 Marshall Cavendish International (Singapore) Private Limited   Primary Mathematics (Standards Edition) Tests 3A

5. Which number belongs in the box?

    □ × 3 × 8 = 216

    A 2   **C** 6

    B 4   **D** 9

6. Divide 5314 by 5.

    A 162 R 1   **C** 1062 R 1

    B 162 R 4   **D** 1062 R 4

7. Kate bought 7 times as much lemonade as Peter.
    Polly bought twice as much as Peter.
    If Peter bought 6 pints of lemonade, how much lemonade
    did they buy in all?

    A 12   **C** 54

    B 42   **D** 60

8. There were 476 adults and 3 times as many children
    at a concert.
    Each adult at a concert paid $9 and each child paid $4.
    How much was collected?

    A $1428   **C** $5712

    B $4284   **D** $9996

9. A table costs 6 times as much as a chair.
    A table and a chair cost $1470.
    How much do 4 chairs cost?

    A $210   **C** $840

    B $245   **D** $980

Primary Mathematics (Standards Edition) Tests 3A

© 2008 Marshall Cavendish International (Singapore) Private Li

Use the graph to answer questions 10 to 12.
The graph shows Mandy's weight over several years.

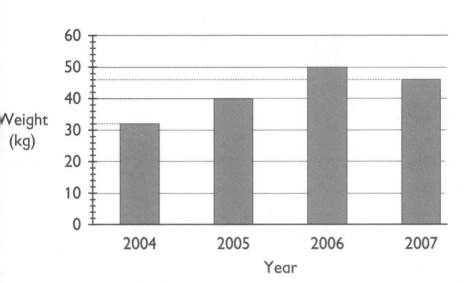

10. What was her weight in 2004?

    A   32 kg   C   47 kg

    B   34 kg   D   50 kg

11. In which year did her weight increase the most?

    A   2004   C   2006

    B   2005   D   2007

12. How much weight did she lose in 2007?

    A   4 kg   C   10 kg

    B   8 kg   D   45 kg

Look at the squares below and answer questions 13 to 15.

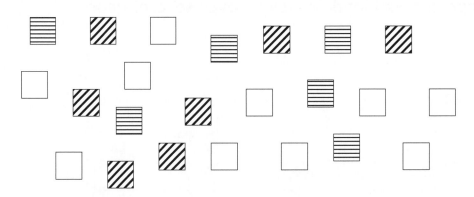

13. Which tally chart shows the correct number of each type of square?

A

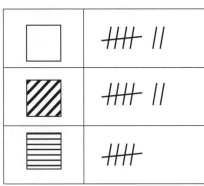

C

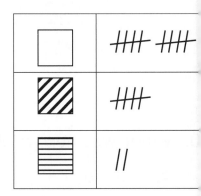

B

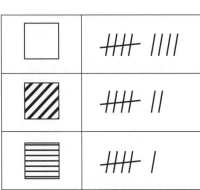

D

☐	‖‖‖ ‖‖‖
▨	‖‖‖ ‖‖
▤	‖‖‖ ‖

14. How many more ☐ than ▨ are there?

A   3   **C**   7

B   4   **D**   10

Primary Mathematics (Standards Edition) Tests 3A   © 2008 Marshall Cavendish International (Singapore) Private Lim

15. How many squares are there in all?

A   13   C   17

B   16   D   23

The tally chart below shows the number of vehicles at a car park. Use the data to answer questions 16 and 17.

Cars	∦∦ ∦∦ ∦∦
Motorcycles	∦∦ ||||
Vans	∦∦ ||||
Bicycles	∦∦ ∦∦ ∦∦ ∦∦ |

16. Which graph represents the above data?

A

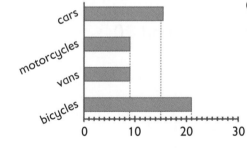

C

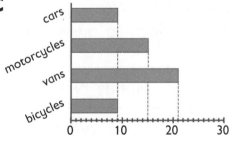

B

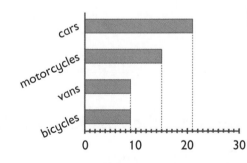

D

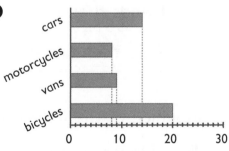

17. Which two vehicles were there the same number of?

A   bicycles and motorcycles   C   bicycles and cars

B   motorcycles and vans   D   vans and cars

© 2008 Marshall Cavendish International (Singapore) Private Limited

18. At a carnival, a mat was colored as shown below.

Red	Red	Yellow
Yellow	Blue	Red
Red	Green	Yellow

Eleanor threw a ring onto the mat.
The ring was _____ to fall on red.

A   certain   **C**   unlikely

B   likely   **D**   impossible

A coin is tossed twice every time and the results are recorded below.
Use the data to answer questions 19 and 20.

Heads twice	5
Tails twice	9
Heads then tails	2
Tails then heads	3

19. In which of the following ways did the toss land the least?

A   Heads twice   **C**   Tails twice

B   Heads then tails   **D**   Tails then heads

Primary Mathematics (Standards Edition) Tests 3A   © 2008 Marshall Cavendish International (Singapore) Private Lim

10. Which graph shows how the coin landed?

A

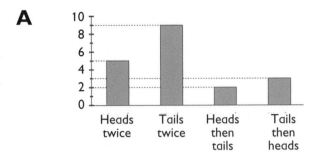

B

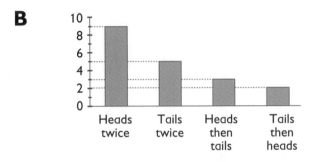

C

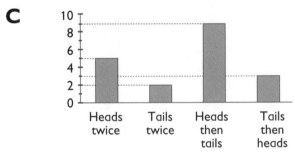

D

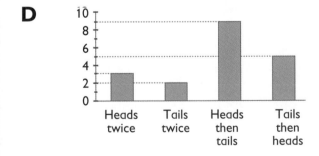

Blank

Answers

Each question is worth 1 point unless otherwise shown in brackets [ ].

Unit 1: Numbers to 10,000

Chapter 1 • Test A

1. 3000 + 800 + 10 + 6
2. 75
3. seven thousand, thirty-five
4. 1002
5. 3429; 3430   [2]
6. (a) 6   [1] (b) 100   [1] (c) tens   [1]
7. >; >
8. 0
9. 7410
10. 897, 1293, 1329, 2329   [2]
11. 237, 273, 327, 372, 723, 732   [2]
12. (a) Accept all possible answers.   [2]
    (b) Answers vary.   [2]

Chapter 1 • Test B

1. C   2. D   3. D   4. B   5. A
6. D   7. A   8. B   9. C   10. C

Chapter 2 • Test A

1. 3407
2. (a) 725   [1] (b) 725; 1000; 1725   [1]
3. 10,000
4. 7402
5. 3360; 3460
6. 3900
7. 1908
8. 1147
9. 6216
10. 2584, 2604, 2614   [2]
11. 7461, 7061   [2]
12. 100; 2975; 3075 or 2975; 100; 3075

Chapter 2 • Test B

1. A   2. A   3. D   4. A   5. C
6. C   7. B   8. D   9. D   10. C

Chapter 3 • Test A

1. (a)

   (b) 40   [1]
2. (a) 1680   [1] (b) 1700   [1]
3. 600
4. 7200
5. 4100
6. 3000
7. 9000
8. 64

9. 1250
10. Any number between 715 and 724
11. thousand
12. 4; any digit from 0 to 9   [2]

Chapter 3 • Test B

1. B   2. B   3. D   4. A   5. B
6. D   7. B   8. B   9. D   10. C

Unit 1 • Cumulative Test A

1. seven thousand, five hundred twenty
2. 2411
3. 6000 + 700 + 8
4. 3033
5. 8000
6. Accept all possible answers.
7. <; <
8. 9999
9. 8572, 8527, 2857, 2785   [2]
10. Any number between 4710 and 4969
11. 4347; 7347   [2]
12. 7018, 7008   [2]
13. 8225
14. 2472   [2]
15. (a) 8020   [1] (b) 8000   [1]
16. 8670
17. 7000
18. 1332
19. Smallest number: 2536   [1]
    Greatest number: 3265   [1]

Unit 1 • Cumulative Test B

1. C   2. D   3. B   4. C   5. D
6. B   7. B   8. B   9. C   10. B
11. B   12. C   13. C   14. D   15. A
16. D   17. B   18. B   19. D   20. A

Unit 2: Addition and Subtraction

Chapter 1 • Test A

1. 2   14. 29
2. 99   15. 146
3. 31   16. 274
4. 78   17. 30
5. 87   18. 328
6. 42   19. 45
7. 16   20. 332
8. 28   21. 380
9. 33   22. 577
10. 64   23. 58
11. 90   24. 91
12. 81   25. 150
13. 124

Chapter 1 • Test B

1. C   2. A   3. D   4. B   5. B

© 2008 Marshall Cavendish International (Singapore) Private Limited

6. A   7. B   8. C   9. C   10. D

Chapter 2 • Test A

1. 15
2. 6
3. 59
4. 100
5. 12
6. 7
7. 53
8. 42
9. –
10. (a) 39 [1] (b) 18 [1] (c) 71 [1] (d) 88 [1]
11. (a) 62 [1] (b) 62; 36; 26 or 62; 26; 36 [1]
12. +, +
13. (a) > [1] (b) = [1] (c) = [1] (d) <, < [1]

Chapter 2 • Test B

1. B   2. A   3. B   4. D   5. A
6. B   7. B   8. D   9. D   10. A
11. A   12. D   13. A   14. B   15. A

Chapter 3 • Test A

1. 117; Estimation: 70 + 50 = 120 [2]
2. 14; Estimation: 80 – 70 = 10 [2]
3. 200 + 500 = 700
4. 300 + 50 = 350; No [2]
5. 800 or 820
6. 500 or 440
7. 836; Addition: 57 + 836 = 893 [2]
8. 862; Estimation: 200 + 400 + 300 = 900 or
   160 + 400 + 300 = 860 [2]
9. 693; 700 [2]
10. Any number from 0 and 4
11. 195; Estimation: 70 + 20 + 20 + 90 = 200 [2]
12. 403; Estimation: 600 – 400 = 200 or
    630 – 400 = 230 [2]

Chapter 3 • Test B

1. A   2. B   3. C   4. D   5. A
6. A   7. D   8. A   9. A   10. D

Chapter 4 • Test A

1. 1144
2. 558
3. 337
4. 148
5. 181
6. (a) 507 [1] (b) 607 [1]
7. (a) 388 [1] (b) 991 [1]
8. (a) 217 [1] (b) 304 [1]
9. (a) 427 [1] (b) 163 [1]
10. (a) 118 [1] (b) 67 [1]

Chapter 4 • Test B

1. D   2. A   3. B   4. A   5. C
6. B   7. B   8. C   9. D   10. C

Chapter 5 • Test A

1. 1634
2. 2813
3. 6; 9 [2]
4. 9067
5. 6020
6. Estimation: 8000 + 1000 = 9000; Yes
7. Estimation: 500 + 700 = 1200; Yes
8. Estimation: 5300 + 3900 = 9200; Yes
9. Circle 7625 – 3998.
10. 4
11. (a) Greatest number: 6431 [1]
       Smallest number: 1346 [1]
    (b) 7777 [1]
12. Check 1834 + 4727 = 6561

Chapter 5 • Test B

1. A   2. D   3. A   4. B   5. B
6. D   7. C   8. A   9. D   10. B

Chapter 6 • Test A

1. 5131
2. 3597
3. 2725
4. 2
5. Addition: 3246 + 1354 = 4600; Yes
6. 4883
7. Estimation: 9000 – 4000 = 5000; Yes
8. 507
9. 3005
10. 4524 – 3796 = 728
11. 5713 [1]
    -1832 [1]
    3881 [1]
12. (a) 827 [1] (b) 507 [1]

Chapter 6 • Test B

1. D   2. A   3. D   4. A   5. A
6. A   7. C   8. B   9. A   10. B

Chapter 7 • Test A

1. 49 [2]
2. 2339 [2]
3. 647 [2]
4. 387 [2]
5. 967 [2]
6. (a) B; 277 [1] (b) 3375 [1]
7. 7000 – 2000 = 5000
   5000 – 3000 = 2000
   Yes [2]
8. 9143 [2]

(a) 1794 [1] (b) Ben; 59 [1]
3232 [2]

apter 7 • Test B

A   2. D   3. C   4. A   5. A
A   7. B   8. A   9. D   10. A

nits 1–2 • Cumulative Test A

five thousand, thirty-six
5000
7215, 3579, 3519, 865   [2]
3279; 3079   [2]
(a) >   [1] (b) >   [1]
9000
334
131
7450
3553
1475
27
4726
5135
734
7624
2827   [2]
1791   [2]
9876   [2]

nits 1–2 • Cumulative Test B

B   2. C   3. B   4. B   5. D
C   7. B   8. C   9. A   10. A
C   12. A   13. D   14. B   15. A
A   17. D   18. A   19. A   20. D

nit 3: Multiplication and Division

apter 1 • Test A

3 × 6 = 18 or 6 × 3 = 18   [1]
3 + 3 + 3 + 3 + 3 + 3 = 18   [1]
6 × $4 = $24   [1]
4 + 4 + 4 + 4 + 4 + 4 = 24   [1]
20
3 × 5 = 15 or 5 × 3 = 15
7
80
2 x 4 = 8   [1]
4 x 2 = 8   [1]
8
3
(a) 0   [1] (b) 1   [1]
. 5; 5   [2]
. (a) ×   [1] (b) −   [1] (c) ÷   [1] (d) +   [1]
. 3 × 3 = 9

Chapter 1 • Test B

1. C   2. C   3. C   4. D   5. D
6. A   7. D   8. A   9. C   10. D
11. B   12. B   13. A   14. C   15. A

Chapter 2 • Test A

1. 70
2. 9
3. 6
4. 15
5. 35
6. 30
7. (a) 10   [1] (b) 3   [1]
8. 16   [2]
9. 12   [2]
10. 12   [2]
11. 8 m   [2]
12. 36 kg   [2]
13. 10   [2]

Chapter 2 • Test B

1. D   2. B   3. C   4. A   5. B
6. B   7. A   8. B   9. B   10. A

Chapter 3 • Test A

1. 108
2. 96
3. 1720
4. 0
5. 6384
6. Estimation: 2000 × 3 = 6000; Yes
7. 9470
8. 95   [2]
9. 351   [2]
10. 2095   [2]
11. 2097   [2]

Chapter 3 • Test B

1. C   2. C   3. D   4. D   5. C
6. C   7. C   8. D   9. D   10. C

Chapter 4 • Test A

1. Draw 4 stars in each circle.   [1]
    (a) 4   [1] (b) 1   [1]
2. Quotient = 3; Remainder = 1
3. No; 18 ÷ 3 = 6
4. 3 × 4 = 12
    12 + 1 = 13
5. 3
6. 19 ÷ 2 = 9 R 1 or 19 ÷ 9 = 2 R 1
7. 2
8. 19   [2]
9. 13; 1   [2]
10. 23 × 4 = 92
    92 + 3 = 95

11. (a) 8 [1] (b) 5 ft [1]
12. 19
13. (a) T [1] (b) F [1] (c) T [1]

Chapter 4 • Test B

1.	C	2.	C	3.	A	4.	D	5.	C
6.	C	7.	C	8.	B	9.	A	10.	C
11.	A	12.	C	13.	C	14.	A	15.	C

Chapter 5 • Test A

1. 300
2. 185
3. 146 × 5 = 730 or 5 × 146 = 730; Yes
4. Quotient = 43, Remainder = 1
5. 30
6. 204
7. 32
8. 599 ÷ 4 = 149 R 3
9. 213, 1
10. 2 [2]
11. 81 [2]
12. 349 [2]

Chapter 5 • Test B

1.	C	2.	C	3.	B	4.	C	5.	C
6.	A	7.	D	8.	D	9.	D	10.	C
11.	B	12.	B	13.	C	14.	D	15.	A

Units 1–3 • Cumulative Test A

1. 500
2. one thousand, nine hundred thirty-two
3. <
4. 568
5. 3905
6. (a) 3207 [1] (b) 1112 [1]
7. >
8. 24
9. 6 [2]
10. 400
11. 236 × 4 = 944; Yes
12. 3156
13. 1
14. 1
15. 145
16. 4 boys and 5 girls [2]
17. 63 x 5 = 315
    315 + 2 = 317
18. 107; 2
19. 105 [2]
20. 288 [2]

Units 1–3 • Cumulative Test B

1.	C	2.	B	3.	D	4.	A	5.	A
6.	B	7.	A	8.	B	9.	C	10.	B
11.	A	12.	D	13.	C	14.	A	15.	D
16.	A	17.	A	18.	C	19.	C	20.	A

Unit 4: Multiplication Tables of 6, 7, 8 and 9

Chapter 1 • Test A

1. 42
2. 9
3. 8; 8 [2]
4. 3 × 6 = 18 [1]
   6 × 3 = 18 [1]
5. 9
6. (a) 6 [1] (b) 6; 54 [1]
7. 1962
8. 5
9. 36 × 6 = 216 or 6 × 36 = 216
10. 1512; Estimation: 300 × 6 = 1800 [2]
11. 1766 [2]
12. 155 [2]
13. 6420 [2]

Chapter 1 • Test B

1.	B	2.	D	3.	C	4.	D	5.	A
6.	A	7.	B	8.	C	9.	D	10.	B
11.	A	12.	C	13.	C	14.	A	15.	C

Chapter 2 • Test A

1.

Number of boxes	1	2	3	4	5	6	7	8	9
Number of pencils	7	14	21	28	35	42	49	56	63

[2]
2. 4 × 7 = 28 [1]
   7 × 4 = 28 [1]
3. 3; 3 [2]
4. (a) 70 [1] (b) 70; 63 [1]
5. 7
6. 42
7. 14 × 7 = 98 or 7 × 14 = 98
8. 2534
9. 1168, 2 [2]
10. 12 [2]
11. 420 [2]
12. 54 [2]

Chapter 2 • Test B

1.	D	2.	C	3.	A	4.	B	5.	B
6.	C	7.	B	8.	A	9.	D	10.	B

Chapter 3 • Test A

1. A is 3. B is 56.
2. 4 × 8 = 32 or 8 × 4 = 32 [1]
   32 ÷ 4 = 8 or 32 ÷ 8 = 4 [1]
3. 8 + 8 + 8 + 8 + 8 + 8 = 48 or
   6 + 6 + 6 + 6 + 6 + 6 + 6 + 6 = 48
4. 24
5. 224 [1]
   Estimation: 30 × 8 = 240 [1]

34 × 8 = 272; Yes
5760
103 R 3
=
802 × 8 = 6416
6416 + 3 = 6419
32 [2]
30 [2]
3024 [2]
267 [2]

hapter 3 • Test B

B 2. C 3. A 4. A 5. D
A 7. C 8. A 9. C 10. B

hapter 4 • Test A

9; 81
8; 8 [2]
63
4 × 9 = 36 or 9 × 4 = 36
80 R 5
1143
Quotient = 1019; Remainder = 8 [2]
Estimation: 500 × 9 = 4500
252 [2]
. 3645 [2]
. 45 [2]
. 57 [2]
. 45 [2]

hapter 4 • Test B

B 2. C 3. D 4. A 5. B
C 7. B 8. D 9. A 10. B

hapter 5 • Test A

2 × 3 × 4 = 24
*Accept 2, 3 and 4 in any combination in the first
three blanks.
(a) 14; 84 [1] (b) 100; 700 [1]
228
1800
(a) 3000 [1] (b) 400 [1]
350 ÷ 7 = 50
Circle 4012 ÷ 9.
198 [2]
(a) 300 [1] (b) 3 [1]
. (a) 560 [1] (b) 60 [1]

hapter 5 • Test B

. B 2. D 3. D 4. D 5. D
. A 7. C 8. C 9. A 10. B
. D 12. D 13. B 14. A 15. C

Units 1–4 • Cumulative Test A

2185, 2815, 5993, 6002 [2]

---

2. 30th July
3. 483
4. 4000
5. 55 − 8 = 47
6. Shade 8 rows of 4 squares or 4 rows of 8 squares.
7. Draw 8 rows of 7 circles or 7 rows of 8 circles; 56
8. 174
9. (a) F [1] (b) F [1] (c) T [1] (d) T [1]
10. 2190
11. =; =
12. 102; 1
13. 781 × 9 = 7029
    7029 + 5 = 7034
14. 36 [2]
15. 496 [2]
16. 50
17. 8 [2]
18. 22 [2]
19. 185 [2]
20. 42 [2]

Units 1–4 • Cumulative Test B

1. B 2. D 3. A 4. A 5. A
6. D 7. D 8. D 9. A 10. A
11. D 12. A 13. C 14. C 15. B
16. B 17. C 18. B 19. A 20. B

Unit 5: Data Analysis

Chapter 1 • Test A

1. (a) Boys [1] (b) 27 [1] (c) 26 [1] (d) 6 [1]
2. (a) plums [1] (b) 25 [1] (c) 160 [1]
3. (a) Charles [1] (b) 16 [1]
   (c) Amy; 4 [1] (d) Charles and Dillon [1]
4.

	Section A	Section B	Total number of questions
Test A	7	14	21
Test B	12	15	27
Total number of questions	19	29	48

[2]

   (a) 6 [1] (b) Section B [1] (c) 54 [1]

5.

Linsy Francis Gerry Harry Janet

[2]

(a) Harry; $15   [1] (b) $3   [1]

6.

Colors	Tally	Number of students
Red	＃＃ ////	9
Blue	＃＃ /	6
Green	＃＃ /	6
Yellow	////	4

[2]
(a) 25   [1] (b) Red   [1] (c) Yellow   [1]

Chapter 1 • Test B

1. B   2. B   3. D   4. A   5. A
6. D   7. B   8. D   9. B   10. B

Chapter 2 • Test A

1. (a) impossible   [1] (b) likely   [1]
   (c) certain   [1] (d) unlikely   [1]
2. (a)

(b) white   [1]
3. (a) white   [1] (b) black, gray   [1]
4. (a) unlikely   [1] (b) impossible   [1] (c) likely   [1]
5. (a) [2]

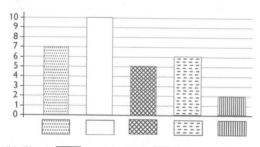

(b) Check ▢   [1] (c) Check ▦   [1]

Chapter 2 • Test B

1. B   2. C   3. B   4. C   5. C
6. D   7. B   8. A   9. A   10. B

1. 8650
2. First box: Any number smaller than 21
   Second Box: Any number greater than 58
3. 14   [2]
4. 6954   [2]
5. 35 ÷ 7 = 5 or 35 ÷ 5 = 7
6. (a) 36   [1] (b) 48   [1]
7. 55
8. 3528

9. by car
10. 9
11. 56
12. 352
13. A; 508
14. 1089
15. 3
16. Insert an 'X' in the '4' column.
17. 16
18. Green
19. (a) unlikely   [1] (b) certain   [1]
    (c) impossible   [1] (d) certain   [1]

1. D   2. B   3. A   4. C   5. [
6. D   7. D   8. D   9. C   10. A
11. C   12. A   13. D   14. A   15. [
16. A   17. B   18. B   19. B   20. A

234

Blank

Blank